Combating Communal Conflict

Perception of Police Neutrality during Hindu-Muslim Riots in India

Combating Communal Conflict

Perception of Police Neutrality during Hindu-Muslim Riots in India

V.N. Rai, IPS

Uttar Pradesh

Manas Publications

New Delhi-110002 (INDIA)

MANAS PUBLICATIONS
(Publishers, Distributors, Importers & Exporters)
4402/5A, Main Ansari Road
(Adjacent Bank of Baroda)
Darya Ganj, New Delhi-110 002 (INDIA)
Off. © 23260783, 23265523, Res. © 23842660
Fax: 011-23272766
E-mail: manaspublications@vsnl.com

New: ISBN 978-81-7049-340-2

Rs. 495/-

Typeset by
Manas Publications

Printed in India by
Nice Printing Press, Delhi
and Published by Mrs Suman Lata for
Manas Publications, 4402/5A, Main Ansari Road
(Adjacent Bank of Baroda)
Darya Ganj, New Delhi-110 002 (INDIA)

Contents

Preface

The track record of the Indian Police in combating communal riots bespeaks of their extremely regrettable performance. Almost every major riot, haunts the minds of the minorities, leaving an indelible imprint. Worst of all allegations is that the behavioural attitude of the Indian Police smacks of communal prejudices. Prejudice against minorities and failure to project them are not allegations made against the police force of any particular State, but against the police force in general. In the minds of minorities, the image of a Policeman is that of an enemy. The concerned police have been accused of committing atrocities on the minorities and of resorting to active inaction so as to allow violence of the majority community to run riot by many commissions of enquiry, objective observers, the media, Human Rights organisations, judiciary and representatives of the minority communities. The Police always react to these accusations by blaming them on the vested interests and incomplete information and trying to get them erased on these grounds. But, the truth cannot be suppressed by ignoring the ground realities and denying the facts. It will surface in no time!

When I, as a fellow of the SVP National Police Academy, Hyderabad, got an opportunity to study the behaviour of Indian Police during communal riots, I did not realise that my work could be so interesting and challenging. The more I got myself immersed in the research, the more I became aware of my limitations. The biggest limitation was the difficulty I experienced in trying to overcome the mental barrier of an average policeman. Many of the police officers and men with whom I had an opportunity to interact were convinced that the most effective way to control or prevent a communal riot, was to adopt harsh measures against the Muslims. Almost all of them, with a very few exceptions, were of the view that Muslims were responsible for starting communal riots and therefore, the most effective way of preventing them from doing so was to deal harshly with that community. Perhaps, this is the reason that events like Hashimpura (1987, Meerut) or Logain (1989, Bhagalpur) where the police killed more than 30 innocent members of the minority community or allowed more than 100 to be slaughtered by those belonging to the majority community, have not been able to create any feeling of repentance and are even justified with forceful arguments. It was this mental barrier that prevented me from gaining access to many police documents that would have helped this study.

As a police officer, it's my firm belief that unless we come to terms with the fact that we have been committing colossal blunders in dealing with communal riots, we will continue to repeat our mistakes. Unfortunately, the police leadership is not prepared to accept these mistakes. I think this is the reason that in spite of the fact that it was the SVP National Police Academy that gave me the fellowship to undertake this study, it refused to publish my findings. But thanks to the LBS National Academy of Administration, Mussoorie, for having taken the initiative in publishing my study. I would specially like to thank Shri N.C. Saxena, LBS National Academy of Administration, Mussoorie, for having taken pain to publish it.

V.N. Rai

1

The Study: Its Relevance

Communalism (in modern context) is perhaps the biggest menace the contemporary plural Indian society is facing. It has threatened the basic value system envisaged in Indian Constitution. India has opted for a secular democracy but, during the last decade or so, our secular polity has constantly been under threat. If the growing communalisation of Indian society and the physical expression of this malaise in communal rioting are not checked effectively in time, the very foundation on which our leaders have dreamt of creating a just, secular and forward looking society, will collapse.

Communalism is not the monopoly of any single community whereas all major and minor religious groups have been affected by it. However, given the territorial pervasiveness of Hindus and Muslims, it is their relationship which is the single most important parameter of Indian communalism today. This does not imply that *ipso facto* all the Hindus and the Muslims or even a majority of them are communal, but the fact remains that sentiments and perceptions of communalists are an important ideological influence on their collective appreciation of each other.

Communalism in Indian society manifests itself in its ugliest form in the violence which explodes in the shape of communal riots in almost all parts of the country at short intervals. Communal violence, for the purpose of this study, means violence against a group or an individual targeted on the basis of a communal identity. The target identification, in most of the cases, is guided by a strong belief that the interests of a community having common religion could be protected and furthered by causing injuries to the members of other religious community. Communal violence need not necessarily be physical. In many cases it may be more psychological than physical. In a theocratic state like Pakistan where minorities are deprived of many rights, and live only as second-rate citizens, it is immaterial that fewer number of cases of physical violence took place because the humiliation and deprivation which the minorities faced in their day to day life may be much more traumatic than physical violence. In India certain communities have to change their food habits, attires or ways to celebrate festivals just to avoid any violent reactions from the other community. In most of the cases the change may appear voluntary but an undercurrent of resistance or feeling of the loss of identity is normally present. This is also a form of communal violence which may in the beginning bruise a community psychologically but to physical violence later on.

It is important to mention that victims of communal ideology may not necessarily participate in rioting. The participants, instigators and sympathisers in communal violence have their own respective interests and justifications. For example, the victims of communal ideology would justify their participation on self-righteous grounds. They may subscribe to the view that their participation in communal rioting would help the realisation of their respective objectives, such as, Hindu Rashtra or Darul Haram or Khalistan.

The police force, state or central, is the first organised institution to face the brunt of communal violence. It is involved very actively in all the three stages *i.e.*, incitement, violence and rehabilitation of victims. Since law and order is a state subject, the state police is first pressed into service to quell a communal riot. After it is found that the local police is not able to control a communal riot, central para-military Forces like CRPF, BSF and ITBP or the Army are called to aid and assist the state law enforcement agencies for carrying out their task.

Since the persons manning the police come from the same society that breeds the germs of communal antagonism, they carry along with them the prejudices, suspicions, fears and hatred prevalent in their community for the other community. They continue to address their co-religionists, as 'we' and members of the other community as 'they' even after joining the police.

It would be expected that the youth joining the police would acquire a common secular identity but experience has proved that most of them retain their Hindu or Muslim identities. Even under *Khaki* they continue to remain Hindu or Muslim.

The role of the police forces in communal rioting is affected by the retention of these separate identities. Although most official investigations have tended to absolve the police from allegations of partisan conduct against Muslims, other studies do suggest that the police may not been have impartial and even handed agency that official accounts have made it out to be. Police in most of the communal conflicts in India has displayed marked bias against minorities. The single largest factor behind this perceptible unfair treatment may be the composition of its officer cadre and other ranks with the dominance of Hindus and the impossibility of immunising them from general social currents. It is unfortunate that instead of becoming an institution that operates as an impersonal instrument of law and order, the police as a social agency has become a third and influential variable in the Hindu-Muslim relationship. The study of various communal riots and the role of police organisations reveal the following:

(a) The representation of minorities in the police is disproportionately less than their percentage of population in the country. A study of BPR & D shows that in some of the most communally sensitive states it is less than 5% (MP 4.2%, Maharashtra 4.2% and UP 4.9%).

(b) Policemen carry the prejudices, fears and apprehensions—real or imaginary—from society to their organisations.

(c) In most of the communal situations the Police did not act fairly or impartially (post-Babri mosque demolition riots of December., 1992 or January. 1993 riots in Mumbai are glaring examples when police reacted differently in two identical situations).

(d) Perceptions of police by the members of the majority community and minority community are different. Muslims perceive the police as their enemies. Often a demand is raised to induct Army or para military forces in place of the state police by the minorities in situations of communal strife. In many cases, a communal riot turns into a battle between the police and the Muslims.

I. The Statement of the Problem

The problem was worded as:

"THE PERCEPTION OF POLICE NEUTRALITY DURING THE COMMUNAL RIOTS BY DIFFERENT STRATA OF SOCIETY"

II. Objectives of Study

The objectives of the study were as follows:

(a) To define the concept of Police Neutrality in communal strife situations.

(b) To study the pattern of police behaviour in a communal riot situation with reference to:

  (i) Use of force by police during communal violence;

  (ii) Communal bias in reporting facts, investigations and prosecution of the cases of communal rioting;

  (iii) Treatment of arrested persons in police custody and;

  (iv) Discrimination in preventive actions.

(c) To study the perception of the following regarding police neutrality :

  (i) Riot victims of minority community;

  (ii) Riot victims of majority community and;

  (iii) Police officials;

(d) To prepare a plan of action to check communal bias in the police during communal riots and;

(e) To evolve training intervention for coping with the problem of police bias during communal riots.

III. Plan and Procedures of the Study

(i) The following major riots, which are of significance from the point of view of studying police neutrality in anticipating and managing the communal riots, were studied in depth:

  1. Kanpur Riot-1931
  2. Ranchi Riot-1967
  3. Ahmedabad Riot-1969

4. Bhiwandi & Jalgaon Riots-1970
5. Banaras Riot-1977
6. Jamshedpur Riot-1979
7. Bhagalpur Riot-1989
8. Meerut Riot-1990
9. Ayodhya Incidents-1992
10. Bombay Riots-1992-93.

The study was conducted in two stages:

In the first instance, a detailed narrative reconstruction was drawn up of the long term and immediate background of each riot: the sequences of its development, and the efforts put in by the law enforcing agencies to quell it.

To reconstruct the development of various riots the reports of different forms of Commissions of Enquiry were studied in detail. Other documentation centres like National Archives, New Delhi, and state archives of Uttar Pradesh and Bihar were consulted for the source materials. Reports of Human Rights activists like PUCL and PUDR were also consulted. Information gathered through these and journalistic sources were supplemented by personal interviews.

In the second stage, detailed interviews were conducted with riot victims in majority and minority communities and retired and serving police officials. The riot victims belong to various parts of the country. The police officials chosen were those who had sufficient exposure to the handling of communal riots. Separate interview questionnaires were drawn up for each category of interviewees.

To analyse the information collected from different sources an interdisciplinary approach was maintained. The purpose was not simply to test the veracity of the interviewees, but to delve deep into the psychological as well as sociological dynamics of communal riots with a view to relate them to the behavioural pattern of policemen and the concept of police neutrality in communal riot situations.

IV. Data Gathering Instruments

The following tools and techniques of data collection were used:

(a) Documents
   - (i) Commission of Inquiry reports
   - (ii) Newspaper clippings/reports
   - (iii) Reports of Human Rights activists
   - (iv) Source materials available in National and various state archives.

(b) Structured interviews with the Directors General, Inspectors General, Deputy Inspectors General and Superintendents of Police.

(c) Structured interviews with subordinate police officers who had sufficient expertise in riot control.

(d) Questionnaire to elicit the views of different strata of society on police neutrality during the communal riots.

V. Sample

The following was the sample of the study.

Sl.	Category	Numbers
1.	Police officers	50
2.	Minority Riot Victims	200
3.	Majority Riot Victims	200

VII. Deliminations of the Study

(1) The study was focused on the perception of the neutrality of the police in communal riots only.

(2) The study was confined to the conflicts between the Hindus and the Muslims.

(3) The observations in the study are based on ten major riots, which occurred between 1931 and 1993.

VII. Definition of Important Terms

(1) Police Neutrality: The largely accepted meaning of the term is impartiality or evenhandedness in the application/ enforcement of law.

(2) Communal Riots: Communal riots mean those clashes between the Hindus and the Muslims, in which they fight against each other by forming warring groups on the basis of religion.

Many a times there is a conflict between the state and one group of citizens. The identity of this group may apparently be religious but this clash would not come under the definition of communal rioting.

(3) Strata of Society: Different segments of society whose identity is determined on the basis of their allegiance to a common religion.

2

Communal Riots: The Historical Perspective

Communalism, as defined by Prof. Bipin Chandra[1], is the belief that because a group of people follows a particular religion, its members have, as a result, common social, political and economic interests. It is the belief that in India, the Hindus, the Muslims, the Christians or the Sikhs form different and distinct communities which are independently and separately structured or consolidated and that the followers of a religion share not only a community of religious interests but also common secular interests that is common political, social and cultural interests. A corollary to this is that not only are the interests of a religious community common, but these are necessarily opposed to the interests of other religious communities.

The distinctive features of the above definition of communalism are enumerated below:

1. It negates the concept of pluralism. In a society like India, where there are many distinct regional identities, it takes the position that despite the multiplicity of languages, food habits, attires or diverse regional economic imbalances, a particular religious community possesses a common identity and has common interests.

2. Communalism always requires an enemy, i.e., members of another community. The members of one community are made to believe that their interests—secular or spiritual—can be protected only by hurting the interests of other communities. The victims of communal ideology assume that it is possible to protect their socio-economic and political interests as members of a religious community.

3. The implicit assumption of a communal identity explanation is that the interests of various groups identified as Sikhs, Hindus, Muslims etc., are conflicting and divergent.

In the Indian context, communalism has primarily come to mean the widespread feelings of suspicion, fear, rivalry, vengeance and violence that exist between the Hindus and the Muslims, The objective of this study is neither to define communalism in the academic sense of the term nor to analyse the social, political, economic or cultural factors that reinforce it. We will confine ourselves to the most important manifestation of communalism, i.e., communal riots. Naturally, the study of riots will make us repeatedly ponder over the reasons for the widespread communalisation of Indian society, the forces responsible for increasing it and its ill effects on civic life. We will confine ourselves to Hindu-Muslim conflicts. The Hindu-Sikh, Hindu-Christian and also conflicts within the Hindu society that have surfaced in recent times are not relevant to our study, therefore reference to them will only be incidental.

Role of Imperialism in Engineering Riots

In India, communal riots have mainly been the result of the desire of the British to suppress the Indian nationalist upsurge in internal conflicts and to maintain their regime by all means—fair and foul. It is not sheer coincidence that during every phase of the national movement in which the Hindus and the Muslims participated together, the graph of communal violence showed a downward trend, perhaps a negative trend. As long as the common struggle remained sharp and the Hindu and the Muslims fought shoulder to shoulder against imperialism, communal rioting was completely halted. But, as and when the movement ended unsuccessfully or was withdrawn by the leadership, the demoralised masses fell victim to the British Policy of 'Divide and Rule' and, instead of fighting against their foreign ruler, got involved in fighting each other. Three important phases of the Indian National Movement bear witness to this phenomenon.

During the First War of Independence of 1857-58, Hindu and Muslim soldiers displayed unprecedented unity against their British officers. Communal riots in the modern sense of the term had taken place in the early 19th century, before this War of Independence. Banaras (1809), Kiol (1820), Moradabad, Sambhal, Kashipur (1833), Shahjahanpur (1837), Bareilly, Kanpur, Allahabad (1837-1852) had witnessed clashes between Hindus and Muslims that car be termed as communal riots. But 1857 and 1858 were two years during which not a single communal riot had been reported. To understand the attitude of British Imperialism and the unity forged between the Hindus and the Muslims, it would be interesting to have a look at some of the incidents that occurred between 1853 and 1855. In 1853 Maulvi Amir Ali, the disciple of the Sufi saint Bandagi Miya of Amethi, received a report in Lucknow that the Babri mosque in Ayodhya had been destroyed and its site had been occupied by members of the Bairagi sect.[2] He tried to meet Wajid Ali Shah, Nawab of Avadh, in Lucknow. When his attempts to meet the Nawab proved fruitless, he gave a call for Jehad from Lucknow. Now, Wajid Ali Shah, disturbed by the call for Jehad, tried to settle the matter peacefully. While the forcible occupation of the site was not given up in spite of his orders, another report reached Lucknow that the mosque had not been destroyed. Meanwhile, Maulvi Amir Ali returned to Amethi from Lucknow and collected a large force of armed Muslims in the name of waging Jehad. Nawab Wajid Ali Shah intervened positively in the events that followed and appealed to the people not to resort to force to settle a religious dispute and also to return the mosque to the Muslims.[3]

According to the treaty signed between Bahu Begum[4] and the British Resident in 1816, the maintenance of peace in Ayodhya was the responsibility of the East India Company. Wajid Ali Shah, therefore, appealed to the British Resident to restrain the Maulvi,[5] but the British refused to take any steps in this direction. The refusal was not on account of any military inability but was motivated by a well-thought out strategy. This strategy was arrived at with an intention to encourage the various issues of disputes between the Hindus and the Muslims in order to prevent them from uniting and throwing away the shackles of slavery. After this, Wajid Ali Shah despatched his own force and after a long and difficult fight, Maulvi Amir Ali, was killed at Shujagunj Bazaar near Heyatnagar. Therefore, in 1855 the elders of the Hindu and the Muslim communities met together at Ayodhya and arrived at a settlement of the problem.

The years 1857 and 1858 witnessed a struggle for freedom in Avadh, the most glorious chapter of which was unity between the Hindus and the Muslims. When this struggle ended unsuccessfully, the conscious efforts made by the British resulted in increasing the Hindu-Muslim divide and distorting the facts regarding the Babri Masjid-Ram Janmabhoomi dispute. The consequences are very clear. The dispute has led to hundreds of riots not only in the 19th Century but right to the present day.

After the struggle of 1857-58, it was in the years 1919 and 1920 that witnessed a tremendous upsurge of popular participation in the *Khilafat* and Non-Co-operation Movements launched against the Rowlatt Act, Jallianwala Bagh massacre and of the Turkish Khalifa. Once again, these movements were examples of unprecedented Hindu-Muslim unity. We find that all over the country, on-going communal riots came to a complete halt during this period. There had been severe riots during the period between 1858 and 1919. Some of these had occurred in places with no earlier history of communal discord and that also were very rare. From the point of view of damage suffered and its far-reaching consequences, the riots in Bareilly (1871), Mau (1893), Mumbai (1893), Nasik (1894), East Bengal (1907), Peshawar (1910), Ayodhya (1912), Agra (1913), Shahabad (1917) and Katarpur (1918) are noteworthy.

The years 1919 and 1920, on the other hand, were remarkably free from rioting. How was it that the rioting of the preceding years came to a sudden halt? The answer to this question is implicit in the riots in 1857 and 1858.

The *Khilafat* movement was a result of the loss of status within the Islamic world of the Turkish Khalifa with the defeat of Turkey and the dismantling of the Ottoman Empire at the end of the First World War. The Muslim obscurantists and fanatics were largely behind this movement. They completely lost sight of the fact that the Khalifa, whose lost prestige they were eager to restore, had become a symbol of oppression and injustice in his own country—Turkey. This is why the moment Mustafa Kemal Ataturk and the nationalist forces led by him abolished the institution of Khalifa, it was welcomed by the Turkish people and, when this happened, the Khilafat movement led by fanatics in a country like India died a natural death.

In spite of the fact that the movement was inherently communal, it helped to forge Hindu-Muslim unity. This unity, however, temporary, also added a glorious chapter to the national movement. The leaders like Mahatma Gandhi saw a golden opportunity to forge Hindu-Muslim unity through this movement and they plunged into it wholeheartedly.

Along with participation in the Khilafat movement, the Congress also started the Non-Cooperation movement all over the country. Both these movements had identical programmes of non-co-operation with the Government. The decision of the Allahabad session of the Khilafat Committee on the 9th of April, 1919, and the resolution of the All India Congress Committee on Non-Co-operation, called upon the people to carry out programmes like resigning from Government jobs, returning of government honours and titles and abstaining from payment of taxes.

The most important feature of the movement of 1919-1920 was the fraternisation of the Hindus and the Muslims. The Hindus forgot their taboos about drink and food and accepted what the Muslims offered. The Muslims invitedthe Hindu leaders to their mosques to deliver addresses. Swami Shradhanand preached at the great mosque of Delhi, Jama Masjid. Gandhi and Sarojini Naidu spoke at the mosque in Mumbai. Muslims identified themselves with the Hindus in the *hartals* and *Satyagraha* and braved the onslaughts of the authorities–*lathi charges*, bullets, imprisonment and loss of property. Satyapal and Kitchlew were the twin leaders of Amritsar; Gandhi and Mohammad Ali jointly directed the national movement.[6]

The effect of Hindu-Muslim unity and its resultant joint struggle had a clear effect on the graph of communal riots occurring in the country. In 1919 and 1920, not a single incident of communal rioting took place. In 1920, the Mopla Revolt took place in Kerala as a result not only of an economic relationship based on inhuman exploitation but also because of the fragility of the well-intentioned attempt to forge Hindu-Muslim unity on a fundamentalist movement like Khilafat The Mopla Revolt is also an interesting study of the way in which economic conflicts are utilised by fundamentalist forces to increase communal polarisation. We will reflect on this later at length in this chapter. But apart from this incident and two minor incidents in Malgaon (1921) and Multan (1922), this period of non-cooperation was free from communal riots.

On the 5th of February, 1922, after the Chouri-Choura police station in Gorakhpur was set on fire, killing all the policemen inside, Gandhiji suddenly withdrew the Non-co-operation movement on the plea that it had turned violent. This sudden withdrawal of the movement left its active participants high and dry, bereft of any programme. The demoralised and directionless mass upsurge once again fell prey to the imperialist policy of divide and rule. Movements like 'Shudhi' and 'Tabliq' were able to attract large sections of the people to their fold. The result of all these is only too clear. In 1923, rioting occurred in 15 to 20 places, the more prominent of which were Amritsar, Lahore and Saharanpur[7]. In 1924, the most horrifying riots took place in Allahabad, Calcutta, Delhi, Gulbarga, Kohat, Lucknow, Nagpur, Jabalpur and Saharanpur, in particular. While the riots of 1923 and 1924 were unprecedented in the toll they took of lives and property, these also demonstrated for the first time that in every geographical part of the country conditions were present that were conducive to the incitement of riots if the Government played the role of encouraging riots rather than suppressing them.

The period of the Civil Disobedience Movement initiated in 1930 is another example of how a turbulent mass upsurge could temporarily overshadow communal divisions and stop communal rioting when it was given a definite programme of action. In 1930, only two riots took place in Mumbai and Dhaka and both were relatively insignificant when compared to the magnitude of earlier riots.

A very significant event of the Civil Disobedience Movement was the refusal of the troops to open fire on the people in Peshawar. The troops were Garhwali Hindus and the agitated people were mostly Muslim Pathans who were being ordered to be shot. This kind of unity can be seen only in movements of this nature. When this movement was withdrawn in March, 1931, the same situation was created that we had seen in 1858 when the Revolt proved unsuccessful, or in 1922, when the Non-cooperation movement was withdrawn. Once again the country was caught in the grip of communal forces. In 1931 itself, there was fierce rioting in Agra, Banaras, Mirzapur and Kanpur. In many ways, the Kanpur riot is especially significant. This was the first major riot that occurred in the United Provinces or Uttar Pradesh of today. Not only did a great patriot and advocate of Hindu-Muslim unity like Ganesh Shankar Vidyrathi lose his life during the riot but according to official figures, about 400 people were killed, more than 1200 injured, 18 mosques, 42 temples and the homes of 248 Hindus and 101 Muslims were destroyed.

The above facts prove conclusively that mass participation in a definite national programme can act as a brake on the activities of communal forces. We must realise the fact that the above-mentioned periods of struggle were very short-lived and were either curbed by the British or withdrawn by their leaders, and so their impact was also very temporary. It would be totally erroneous to conclude that communal forces were crushed by the events of the three periods that we have discussed earlier (1857-58, 1920-22, and 1930). In all these years, aided and abetted by government effort, both Hindu and Muslim communalists were actively engaged in their propaganda and mobilisation of rioters. Especially between the period of 1920–30, the maximum expansion of the forces representing Hindu and Muslim communalism took place, but because of the involvement of vast masses of people in national programmes, they could not recruit enough volunteers to engineer riots. That is why the necessary component for their existence—rioting on communal lines and issues—is absent during these periods. If only efforts at forging Hindu-Muslim unity had concentrated on economic, political and social issues as instruments for mass mobilisation against imperialism, rather than on religious issues like *Khilafat* and cow protection, the fate of the struggle against communal forces would have been quite different.

Difference Between Religious Conflicts and Communal Riots

The argument that communalism and its destructive manifestation—rioting, the evolution of imperialism can lead to dangerous over-simplification. How far is it true to say that communalism in the modern sense developed only after the British came to India and became an effective military and political reality when, in fact, the points of contention, mostly based on religion between the two communities, had already existed? How far is the legacy of medieval history of India, when the Hindus and the Muslims came into conflict with each other on religious and other issues, responsible for the creation of communalism? Is it not a fact that even before the advent of the Muslims in India, there existed active reasons for conflicts between different beliefs (Brahmin/ Bhuddhist; Shaiva/Vaishnava)? To avoid over-simplification, it is necessary to answer some of these questions. Since this study deals primarily with communal riots, these questions will be studied in that context.

Two arguments are given to limit the role of imperialism in the engineering of riots. According to the first, it is wrong to ascribe riots to the British because riots took place in India even before the arrival of the British and were a regular feature of Indian life. According to the second argument, if communal riots were a product of imperialism, then they should have disappeared with the British. However, riots have become an even more regular occurrence and the quotient of violence has increased after the departure of the British.

To re-inforce the first argument, British official records and historians like Christopher Bailey have furnished some evidence. In the Banaras Gazetteer of 1907, a description of the 1809 riot begins in the following fashion,[8] "The only disturbance of the public peace occurred in 1809 and the following year, when the city experienced one of those convulsions which had so frequently occurred in the past owing to the religious antagonism of Hindu and Musalman sections of the society." The Gazetteer does not mention any other riot as example of the 'convulsion'. This task is left to historians like Christopher Bailey.

In this work, *The Pre-History of Communalism: Religious Conflict in India, 1700-1860*, Bailey puts forward a theory of the continuity of communal riots. According to him, the tradition of communal skirmishes was much older than the effective British intervention in Indian society. He mentions many incidents which, according to him, resemble the communal riots of colonial times. He mentions the revolts of Hindu and Sikh peasants against their Muslim landlords in the Seventeenth Century and compares them with riots that took place in Eastern UP in the 1920's and in East Bengal in the 1930's and 40's. If we judge the examples given by Bailey against the normally accepted definitions of communal rioting, we will have an interesting insight into how facts can be distorted in an academic exercise attempting to convert prejudice into reality. Not a single example given by Bailey can be said to be a riot in the communal sense of the term. All the examples cited by him, have the resonance not of communal riots, but of the various economic, political and social rivalries and attempts to influence each other that any composite society of plural beliefs encompasses. These were basically conflicts and not communal riots. Here, we will have to differentiate between the two.

Religious conflicts are the expressions of the other worldly beliefs of believers. Every religion teaches its followers that its understanding and interpretation of God, prophet, incarnations of God and the Holy Book is the best and the ultimate. According to every religion its Book is sacred. All religions deprive their followers of internal democracy and discourage dissent. They propagate the tremendous faith in one's religious beliefs and a feeling that non-believers are misguided people who lack proper guidance as regards the correct path. Lack of proper knowledge in non-believers leads to conflicts which may be termed as religious conflicts. The Hindu-Muslim conflicts of pre-British fall come under this category. Normally, the destruction of places of worship of other religionists and forced or voluntary conversions were supposed to be part of religious duty. A theological state would include such acts in the charter of its duties along with secular activities like maintaining law and order or realising taxes. The latter part of the state's concern compelled Muslim rulers to keep Hindu officials in top civil and military positions in their government. It was basically a self-preservation instinct which had encouraged many Muslim rulers to ban practices like cow-slaughter. The famous advice of Babar at the time of his death, to his son Humaun that the future emperor should keep Hindus in good humour is another example of this instinct.

The democratisation of political institutions and opening of new avenues in the form of government jobs heralded a new era of competitive relationship between the Hindus and the Muslims. During the Colonial period, elections to municipal committees in the last decades of the 19th Century, exposed, Indian society for the first time, to a situation where counting of heads and not the sword would be the basis of sharing of power. This led to mobilisation on communal lines. Also the introduction of English as medium of official work led to a situation where Muslims found themselves totally outwitted by the Hindus who had no inhibitions in adopting western education. These two factors were responsible for new areas of conflicts between the two communities. These were worldly conflicts confined to issues like representation in elected bodies, medium of transacsation in courts or government jobs. With the active help of British imperialism, the communal organisations were able to convince their co-religionists that the solution to these non-religious issues was available in religion. This was the basic cause of widespread communal rioting between the two communities.

The basic difference between religious and communal conflicts could be found in the involvement of civil population in rioting. During the period of the Muslim state, the conflict was normally between the state and the civil Hindu population. The state would destroy places of Hindu worship, impose taxes like Jizia or encourage conversion, but the relationship between Hindu and Muslim populations living side by side, would continue to remain cordial. Since the state had its own army, it had no need to mobilise armed or violent mobs to harm the other segment of society. The state also had no crisis of legitimacy. The typical competitive relationship during the British period resulted in clashes between the Hindu and the Muslim civil populations. The communal organisations would need to mobilise mobs to attack each other by inciting them on non-religious issues. In this situation, the state would choose to appear neutral. The issues raised by these organisations and large scale mobilisation of the people to achieve communal objectives, helped such organisations in gaining legitimacy by posing themselves as the real representatives of their respective community.

Before the British presence in India became effective, we find evidence of only one incident of Hindu-Muslim conflict that can be termed as a riot. This occurred in Ahmedabad in 1713. According to Khafi Khan, a contemporary historian, a Hindu, in spite of protests from his Muslim neighbour, insisted on burning 'Holika' in their common compound. This dispute was taken to a Muslim officer for settlement and he gave his decision in favour of the Hindu who proceeded to burn 'Holika'. The next day, the Muslim sacrificed a cow in honour of the Prophet in front of his house. This enraged the Hindus in the neighbourhood and they attacked the Muslims in the vicinity. In the ensuing struggle, the fourteen-year old son of the Muslim, who had sacrificed the cow, was killed. In retaliation, a Muslim mob collected and aided by Afghan soldiers, entered the fray. In the rioting that went on for the next three or four days, many persons belonging to both communities were killed and much property was damaged. Leaders of both communities then appealed to the ruler to restore peace.

The written account of this riot is the first one in which all the elements of a communal riot are to be found. How the examples cited by Bailey differ from this can be understood only when we understand the relationship between the state and its citizens, the relations between different groups of citizens and the nature of the state in medieval times.

Several historians resort to extreme positions while writing about medieval history or the history of Muslim rule and of Hindu-Muslim relations during the period. On the one hand, are historians like Mohd. Yasin,[9] according to whom the greater part of the Mughal period saw tolerance, sympathy and mutual affection between the Hindus and the Muslims. According to other extremist historians, the Muslim period of Indian history is equated with Muslim atrocities (idol-breaking, rape, forced conversion, jizia, oppression, loot and massacre) and intolerance. While a detailed study of the history of the period is not contemplated here, a look at some of these trends will help us in our present study.

When Hindu-Muslim relations are being analysed, the idol-breaking facet of Muslim rule is often held responsible for the bitterness that even now agitates Hindu historians them. From a historical point of view, it cannot be denied that many Muslim rulers did destroy Hindu temples. It would, however, be an over-simplification of facts to claim that only intolerance or fanaticism was responsible for this destruction of temples. Generally, Hindu temples were destroyed because of greed for gold, silver and jewels stored in them. This was the reason for Mahmud of Ghazni's attack on the Somnath temple to reach which he had to travel hundreds of miles, leaving thousands of temples untouched on the way.

It is also a fact that it was not only the Muslim rulers who fell prey to the greed for wealth. Many Hindu rulers also looted and destroyed temples. Harsha, the king of Kashmir, was one such who created a separate department to plunder temples and bring the looted property to the government exchequer.[10]

Yet another reason for the destruction of temples was the political gain it brought. By destroying a symbol of its beliefs, the conqueror created a psychological climate for acceptance of its subjugation by the defeated populace. This is the universal method by which the enemy's morale is destroyed. In India itself, the number of Jain and Buddhist temples destroyed by Brahmin kings is perhaps greater than the number of temples destroyed by the Muslims. Once their rule was formally and truly established, the number of temples destroyed by the Muslims fell. The logic behind this was that once their rule was unanimously accepted, the need for destroying temples ceased to exist.

The attitude of the Muslim state towards its subjects was no different from that of any other state. It was more concerned about its own survival than the propagation of any religion. The Muslim rulers displayed more concern for the collection of revenue and maintenance of their military might. That is why various dynasties of Muslim rulers gave high posts to the Hindus in their revenue and military administration. By the time of the Mughals the proportion of the Hindus in the army and revenue departments had risen considerably because, by then, the opposition to Muslim rule had declined substantially. It is no accident that the Mughal armies that fought the two symbols of opposition. Maharana Pratap and Shivaji—were themselves led by Rajput Generals and officers.

Without going into a detailed analysis of Muslim rule, the above facts have been mentioned only to understand the nature of the relations between the state, predominantly Muslim and its subjects, predominantly Hindu, in medieval India. The establishment of a nation state in India became possible only in the beginning of the 19th Century. Till then, each existing centre of power was involved with its geographical expansion. The Muslim rulers were also involved with this. For about 500 years, Delhi was the centre of their power and they had to make continuous efforts to extend it in every direction, wherever possible. As a result of this attempt they had to confront different opposing forces in different periods of time. Usually, a conflict between two kingdoms took place. Sometimes both were Muslim-ruled and more often, one Muslim ruled and the other was a Hindu-ruled. Usually, the participation of the people in these conflicts was minimal. Relations between the Hindus and the Muslims in remote villages and towns remained unaffected.

While analysing the facts presented by Christopher Bailey, it is necessary to compare the omnipresence of the state in the daily lives of its citizens in Muslim and British times. The colonial British state was "not only far more modern, powerful, centralised and interventionist than any state that had existed before in the subcontinent, it is (was) far more self-consciously neutral—standing above society, and not really part of it—than any previous state, a position that no previous state had especially claimed or desired."[11]

In the medieval period, the state did not directly interfere with the day to day life and social observance of its citizens. Especially when it was geographically vast, it limited its control and interaction with its distant citizens to the collection of revenue and through this to the administrative structure of the recognition of its authority. The vast kingdom was extremely loose and, in fact, the local satraps enjoyed more influence than the central authority. As long as the local satraps, collected and paid revenue and did not shirk their responsibility in times of war, the relations between them and the central authority remainedproper and cordial.

Colonial British rule completely changed this balance of relationships. After the Battle of Plassey in 1757, British rule began to make its official presence felt in different parts of India in different ways. By 1857, the state had started intervening in everyday life through various institutions. Troops of the Bengal, Chennai and Mumbai Presidencies were stationed in cantonments all over the country. Means of communication like telegraphy became widely used. In 1847, the East India Railway Company was formed and, in the next few years a huge network of railway lines was laid. The railways were introduced not only to transport raw cotton out of India and finished cotton goods imported from England in and around the country, but also to facilitate the rapid movement of troops.[12] That is why military experts were consulted before the laying of the lines and determination of their gauges. The Revolt of 1857 demonstrated how helpful the railways were in state intervention. If the Calcutta-Ranigunj line (120 miles) had not been laid and had Col. Neill not been able to load his troops in the train to Ranigunj in time,[13] then definitely the British troops in the cantonment of Banaras, Allahabad and Kanpur would have had to face even greater difficulties.

The existence of a uniform system of policing and law enforcement in British India made the existence of the state more stable and its intervention more effective. The legislation in 1861 of the Police Act, the Indian Penal Code and the Criminal Procedure Code created instruments which helped to establish a Nation State in the modern sense of the term and also brought the state to the door-step of every citizen. The creation of a bureaucracy for revenue collection placed a representative of the state in every village.

The new state was not merely more interventionist than the Medieval state, it was also more insensitive. There are several concrete examples regarding of its lack of sensitivity. The Muslim rulers, with a few early exceptions, had made India their home. They were neither interested in carrying the wealth of India away to a distant place nor were they interested in ruling India from far away centres through representatives. The compulsion of living and dying in this country and, therefore, of co-existence with the local people made it necessary for them to concern themselves with the welfare of their subjects. On the other hand, lack of these factors and competition with Indian producers in the economic sphere compelled British rulers to destroy local handicrafts and industries and also to create a state which, while it remained aloof and alienated from its citizens, continued to interfere in their lives in an insensitive fashion. Edmund Burke, while comparing the two states, has observed quite rightly that the British state had only impoverished the Indian people.

It is this difference in attitude between Muslim and British rule that forced the latter to adopt instruments like the maxim of 'Divide and Rule'. Immediately after the Rvolt of 1857, Elphinstone summed up the colonial point of view by saying 'Divide ET Imperial was the old Roman motto as it should be ours'. The Muslim State did not need to divide the people to rule.

The logical culmination of 'Divide and Rule' was communal conflict and that is what the state's conscious effort produced. Earlier, a Muslim king and a Hindu one would fight each other and armies and commanders on both sides would be both Hindus and Muslims and the relations between the civilians—Hindus and Muslims—would remain unaffected. But now while the state had made itself expansionist and mercenary to a large extent, its policies and efforts made Hindus and Muslims fight each other. A little later, we shall dwell upon how the British colonial rule used 'Active Inaction' to engineer riots. First, we should search for an answer to the argument that if the British were responsible for the phenomenon of communal riots, why it still persists even after British rule has ended. This argument is the result of inadequate appreciation of concrete realities. We must remember that we became independent in the background of tragic communal happenings. The partition of the country was the result of many factors like separate electorates, rise of Muslim League and organisations like Hindu Mahasabha, increased communal polarisation and horrifying communal rioting. Lakhs of people died during partition and crores were uprooted from their homes. The continuance of communal riots even after the departure of British may be attributed to the sad memories of partition as well as class character of most of the non-left political parties which may never fail to engineer a communal riot if it politically suits them. We will be discussing the reasons of communal riots after departure of British in detail in the next chapter.

British State—An Abettor to Communal Rioting

While studying the contribution of the British to fomenting communal rioting, it would be useful to look at some written historical evidence of pre-British times. During the medieval period, Hindu-Muslim relations often went through periods of tension which, with the state's active connivance, could have caused ugly ramifications in the years to come. The first reference to such tension could be found in Ibn Batuta's Travels.[14] He describes the Muslim settlement of 4000 families near Manjasur (perhaps Mangalore) in South India in the early 15th Century during the reign of Ramdas. He describes frequent conflicts between these Muslims and other citizens and the active role of the king in maintaining peace because he realised the commercial importance of the Muslims. We can well imagine that if the state encouraged these conflicts or if it considered soaring dissension between the followers of different faiths as being essential to its own existence, then these conflicts would have developed into communal riots.

We have already referred to the first communal riot in the modern sense of the term, the Ahmedabad riot of 1713.

In this riot also, we do not find the active participation of the state. While it is true that the Afghan troops stationed there came to the help of their co-religionists, it is equally true that senior citizens of both communities approached the ruler King to restore peace because they believed that he was interested in doing so.

In his book *Tarikh-e-Hindi*[15] written in 1759, Rustam Ali describes a conflict in Delhi that contained within it seeds of a major communal riot. A Hindu named Subhakaran killed a Muslim in the month of Shaban and there was an uproar in the Jama Masjid as the Muslims demanded revenge. Some royal servants sided with the Hindus. On a Friday, rioting took place and, in the masjid area. Seventeen people were killed and a steward of the king, Sher Afghan Khan, was wounded. He was saved by Roshan-ud-Daula. Although Rustam Ali does not describe the causes of the riot, it is apparent from the rioting that there must have been some major cause behind such a conflict. And still, in spite of the fact that an important government functionary was seriously wounded, the rioting did not spread, nor did it last for more than one day and neither did the state encourage it in any way.

However, there were some other examples of the role of the British Government. Suffice it to restrict ourselves to examining only three examples. The three incidents took place in three different periods after the establishment of effective British rule. These are the attitude of the government towards the Babri Masjid-Ramjanambhoomi dispute after the revolt of 1857-58, the role of the administration during the 1931 Kanpur riots, the refusal of the British bureaucracy to halt the killing during Direct Action of 1946 in Calcutta. An analysis of these three incidents will undoubtedly help us to understand the role of the British government in encouraging communal rioting.

It is no coincidence that the first reference to the Babri Masjid-Ramjanambhoomi dispute or to the destruction of the Ramjanambhoomi temple and the construction of the Babri Masjid on its site should be made in the Faizabad *Gazetteer*, composed by H.R. Neville. Abdul Fazal, the author of *Ain-e-Akbari*, who was active during the period that the destruction of the temple and the construction of the mosque were supposed to have taken place, and the greatest devotee of Ram, Goswami Tulsidas, who was also a contemporary, had never described such an incident. It is Nevile who writes that the debris of the destroyed monument (temple) were used to build the new monument (mosque)[16]. It is only in the 19th Century that the story of the temple being broken to construct a mosque became prevalent and was mentioned in the government documents. These arguments were later treated as historical facts and propagated as such.[17] While there is no historical evidence in support of the assertion that the temple was demolished, it seems likely that part of the area was used by the Hindus for prayers.

According to the first European traveller, William Finch who visited Ayodhya between 1608 and 1611, within the premises of the Babri Masjid, Hindus were free to pray and perform their rituals.[18] In spite of this arrangement, there is no historical document that mentions any bloody conflict taking place here. We have already discussed in detail the earliest description of the conflict over the site—the conflicts of 1853 and 1855. We have seen how the responsibility of restraining Maulvi Amir Ali after his declaration of Jehad rested with the British according to the terms of the Treaty of 1816. A suitable agreement arrived at between elders of both the communities–Hindus and Muslims. Perhaps this was the arrangement discussed by William Finch and about which Benet wrote. It is said that upto that time (before the revolt of 1857) the Hindus and the Mohammadans alike used to worship in the mosque-temple.[19]

It would not be out of place to state here that the Nawabs of Avadh contributed greatly to the development of Ayodhya as a religious centre. Ayodhya emerged as an important pilgrimage site in the 18th Century for the first time. Nawab Safdarjung's minister Raja Diwan Rai repaired many temples and built several new ones. Nawab Asafuddaulah's minister, Tikait Rai, contributed substantially to the construction of Hanumangarhi temple. According to Peter van der Veer, the Nawab's Muslim courtiers regularly contributed funds to Hindu priests and religious institutions.[20]

Peter van der Veer, Michael Fisher and J.R.I. Cole[21] have studied contemporary records and conclusively proved that it was the downfall of Wajid Ali Shah and the rise of the British power that aggravated the Ayodhya dispute and turned it into a festering sore that troubles Indian society even today. The Ayodhya dispute was most useful to the British policy of 'Divide and Rule' because fundamental differences of Indian society lay embedded within it. This is why British not only kept the dispute alive but spared no effort in aggravating it.[22]

The Kanpur Riot of 1931

The Kanpur riot of 1931 is important because in terms of loss of life and property it was the biggest riot of its time. According to the official reports, 290 people died in this riot (108 Hindus, 116 Muslims and 66 whose religion could not be determined) and 947 (368 Hindus, 292 Muslims and 305 undetermined) were wounded. In addition, about 50 corpses were either thrown in the rivers or canals or burnt.[23] According to non-official sources, more than 500 persons were killed. Rough estimates of the damage caused to property ran into Rs. 50 lakhs. Some 1700 criminal cases connected with the riots were registered—84 murder cases, 81 cases of attempt to murder, 1203 cases of dacoity, 74 cases of loot and 91 cases of rioting. As many as 29 temples, 18 smaller Hindu shrines and 26 mosques were damaged.

All the destruction occurred in just four days. Rioting started in the afternoon of 24th March, its intensity increased from the morning of 25th. On the 25th, 26th, 27th & 28th, the riot raged intensely. By the 29th and then the 30th, it slowed down and finally ended. During this riot, a nationalist leader of the stature of Ganesh Shankar Vidyarthi, who was equally popular among both Hindus and Muslims, was killed.

Two commissions were set up to enquire into the riots. The official commission presided over by M. Keen, Member, Board of Revenue, had as its members G.L. Allen, District Judge, Agra, Pandit Baldev Ram Dave, Chairman, Improvement Trust, Allahabad, and Nawabzada Mohd. Liyaqat Ali, Member of the United Province Legislative Assembly. In addition to this commission, the Congress party also set up its own commission of Enquiry. Purushottam Das Tandon, Khwaja Abdul Majid, T.A.K. Shervani, Jafarul Mulk and Pandit Sundarlal were nominated to this commission, but T.A.K. Shervani and Khwaja Abdul Majid expressed their inability to serve on the commission for personal reasons. They were replaced by Mazar Ali Sokhta and Abdul Latif. Because government officials refused to depose before this commission, members of the Congress boycotted the official commission. The statement recorded by both the Commissions contain interesting comments on the inclination displayed by the government in not-controlling the riot.

Deposing before the Government commission, the Divisional Commissioner of Allahabad, Kunwar Maharaj Prasad, District Magistrate of Kanpur J.F. Sale and the Supdt. of Police of Kanpur, E.M. Rogers, were unanimous in their opinion that the sole reason behind the fact that the riot could not be controlled was lack of sufficient police force in Kanpur. Later on, the Enquiry Commission concurred with this in its final report. However, other opinion expressed before the commission and the record placed before it by officials, have another tale to tell.

While analysing the statement given before the official commission, it must be kept in mind that those giving the statements were mostly government loyalists.

If Raj loyalists themselves stated that the police were idle spectators to the rioting, then we must accept this as the truth and fathom the reasons for the police attitude.

Statements made by army officers, Anglo-Indians, Hindus, Muslims, traders and mill owners—all mention the suspicious role of the administration during the first days of the riot. In fact, on the 25th and 26th, the worst days of rioting the military was not properly used because of bureaucratic differences on its role and pattern of deployment.

While deciding whether it was the insufficiency of police force available that was responsible for the uncontrolled rioting or whether the administration lacked the will to do so, we will have to examine the reasons given by the District Magistrate, the Superintendent of Police and the Asstt. Superintendent of Police to the commission for failing to act effectively against the rioters. When these officers were repeatedly asked by the members of the commission why they failed either to arrest rioters or to fire upon them, they replied that since rioters would escape into the narrow lanes and by-lanes after incidents of stabbing, arson and stone throwing, it was not possible to apprehend them because of the insufficient number of policemen available. However, witnesses other than the police officers and magistrates stated that the police simply watched incidents of arson and murder taking place, without intervening at all.

The seriousness displayed by the police can be understood by looking at Appendix-I, to the written statement given by Superintendent of Police E.M. Rogers to the commission. This appendix contains a list of incidents of police firing. According to this, they resorted to firing on 13 occasions during the rioting. But on six occasions the fire resorted to was in self-defence after rioters attacked the police, on three occasions it was resorted to protect official residences by the security guards on duty and only on four occasions did firing take place to quell rioting. In a riot, in which according to official reports, about 300 persons were killed, the Superintendent of Police himself accepted that only one rioter was killed in police firing.[24]

It is clear from the statement of Rogers and other officers, that the rioters were in no way anxious for a confrontation with the police or the military. What was lacking was the determination on the part of the police in dealing with them. How the police was actually dealing with them becomes apparent from the statement recorded by the witnesses who deposed before the Congress Commission of Enquiry headed by Dr. Bhagwan Das.

At the time that the residence of the Secretary of the Congress Committee, Piareylal Agarwal, was being looted, "the city Kotwal was personally present at a distance of about 50 to 60 yards from Piareylalji's house. Pitambar Lal Agarwal and Mahabir Ojha told the Kotwal that Piareylal's house was being looted and requested him to save it. But the Kotwal paid no heed."[25]

The Station Officer, Kotwal Ramkaran Singh was reportedly standing by while shops belonging to the Muslims in the Chowk Bazar were being looted. The Muslim shopkeepers repeatedly surrounded him and begged him to intervene and save them from plunder, but he did not do anything. When the bigest trader in hosiery of the United

Province, Abdul Haq, saw his shop being looted, "he with folded hands and putting his cap on In-charge's feet and thus appealing to him to save his shop, but he smilingly turned his face to the reverse side."[26] At that time Ramkaran Singh was accompanied by a Deputy Magistrate, but Abdul Haq's pleading had no effect on either of them.[27]

Both the enquiry commissions corroborate the fact that the cause of the rioting was not non-availability of police force but the attitude of the official machinery which went beyond mere inactivity and actually encouraged rioters.

The Calcutta Riot–1946

The riot that occurred in Calcutta in the course of the Direct Action Day, organised in 1946 by the Muslim League Government of Bengal, is important for this study for many reasons. By this time, it had become obvious that India would shortly become independent and that the responsibility for controlling the riots rested largely with Indians. A large section of the bureaucracy, however, was still British. The amount of control exercised by the elected representatives on ICS and IP officers was practically nil. The military which could have been used effectively along with the civil administration to stop the rioting was outside the control of the elected representatives. The British administration continuously refused to co-operate with the elected government in order to prove not only that it could not control the rioting, but that Hindus and Muslims fought each other any way, and that this would increase after the British left.

This riot is unique in a sense that the forces which were responsible for the riot were in power and when they tried to stop the rioting they failed mainly because of the lack of co-operation of the police and the military. When the rioting started on 16th of August, Muslims were in a dominant position but this situation changed very fast. In a few hours, a frightening massacre of Muslims began. Prime Minister Suhrawardy and the members of his Muslim League Cabinet ran from pillar to post to get logistic and operational support from the British bureaucracy to quell the riots, but failed miserably.

The memoirs of P.S. Mathur published in the *Illustrated Weekly of India* of 19th August, 1973, give an interesting account of the kind of co-operation received by the Muslim League Government from British police officials and the military. Mathur had been a senior officer in Bengal at that time and had access to the inner corridors of the Government. He throws some interesting light on the stubborn attitude of the British Police Commissioner at that time, Hardwick. According to him, when a call came to the Commissioner to send some European sergeants meaning the Anglo-Indian members of the city police force... he would tell the caller in cool and calculated voice *"Kya Bolega, Mister, aap jo mangta hai, us rekam ka sergeant to app ki hi hukum ke saath India quit kar gaya."* (What should I say, Mister, the type of sergeants you are demanding, have left India with your orders). On another occasion, when someone wanted help, he replied, "who am I to interfere in your affairs. The Hindus want us to get out. The Muslims want us to leave the country to them. I am so helpless. Why not ring the Congress Office?"

A senior IP officer and retired Inspector General of Police, UP, N.S. Saxena, had defined the relations between the administration and the government of the time in the following manner. "In fairness to the Muslim League Chief Minister of Bengal, it may be said that he pressed for the Army to be called out but the European administrators opposed the idea and the Army was not called out though it was available. This example is enough to show as to what havoc can be created if the administration at the top is not properly motivated."[28]

The efforts on the part of the British officials to divide their Hindu and Muslim subjects could be well understood by the perusal of a letter from George Couper, Secretary to the Chief Commissioner of Oudh, to G.F. Edmonstone, Secretary to the Government of India, dated Lucknow, Dec. 1st, 1857. This letter, which is available on Appendix-C, clearly shows the frustration of the British officials who were unable to incite Hindus of Bareilly against Muslim rebels who were participating in the Revolt.

While the encouragement given by the British in 1858 to fan the Babri Masjid-Ramjanambhoomi dispute and the failure to stop the rioting in Kanpur in 1931 revealed British efforts to aggravate Hindu-Muslim contradictions as a part of their Divide and Rule policy, their refusal to help the elected government in 1946 in Calcutta reveals their extreme inhibition to accept the fact that power was slipping out of their hands. They were determined to preserve the illusion that after the departure of the white rulers, the country would be in ruins. While expressing their dismay and doubts about the ability of the Indians to sort out their religious and ethnic problems, they lost sight of the fact that it was they, the colonial rulers, who had, in fact, been responsible for the introduction of communalism and communal rioting in India in the first place. To understand the extent to which the British were convinced that their departure would bring to India its worst disaster, it would be interesting to read the speech of the then British Prime Minister Winston Churchill in the Parliament on December. 12, 1946, that refers to the ugly riots of Bihar in 1946. He describes the event as "only the first few drops of rain before the thunderstorm breaks...a foretaste of what may well come in the future."

Churchill intentionally forgot to mention in his speech that it was the machination of the British imperialism that led to the stormy future he was predicting for India.

Exploitation of Economic Issues by Communal Forces

An important cause of communalism and the communal riots springing from it has been unbalanced or exploitative economic relations in Indian society. We find attempts at altering the balance of regional economic realities through political means. Very often, communal forces exploit the economic backwardness of their community to mobilise it against another community. Political and religious goals are usually the hidden motives behind these attempts. Mostly, what appears to be a purely economic movement is really motivated by religio-political objectives about which, those participating in the movement, except for the few leaders, are totally ignorant. They do not realise till the very end how they are being cunningly manipulated by a group of vested interests. The Moplah Revolt of Kerala, Bengali Muslims' struggle against Hindu landlords and The Cow Protection Movement are examples of this kind.

The Moplah Revolt: It sounds incredible but it is true that it was the *Khilafat* and the non-cooperation movement which gave birth to the Moplah revolt of 1921-22. It is also true that the real reasons of the revolt were also to be found in the terrible exploitation on which agrarian relations in the Malabar region were based. These agrarian relations had been responsible for the conflicts between Moplahs and their Hindu and English oppressors that occurred between 1836 and 1919. The 1921-22 Moplah revolt differed from these earlier conflicts in the sense that it ended British rule in an area of hundreds of square kilometres for several months. In addition to being anti-imperialistic, this struggle also had a communal character. According to official records, in Ernad alone, 300 temples were destroyed and 900 Hindus were forcibly converted to Islam. About 20,000 Hindus were forced to flee their homes while those killed included several thousands. It is interesting to examine how an anti-imperialistic struggle assumed a basically communal character.

Before independence, the northern part of what is now Kerala formed the Malabar district of the Madras Presidency. Malabar formed a strip of land that ran parallel to the Arabian sea from north to south. It was 150 miles in length and its width never exceeded 70 miles. The Hindus of Malabar, socially entrapped in an inflexible and unchanging caste system, made up 66 per cent of the population according to the census of 1921.[29] The Namboothiris came at the top of the Hindu caste hierarchy. According to the census, the Namboothiris numbered only 20,000 in a total population of 31 lakhs. Of the population, 32 per cent consisted of Muslims. They spoke Malayalam and were actually the real Moplahs.

Except for a very few, all of them were converted Hindus. According to the censuses of 1901 and 1911[30] only five to six per cent of the population of Malabar was land-owners. Among these, Muslims were almost non-existent. Among the Hindus, the major part of the land was owned by the Namboothiri Brahmins. According to Innes, Collector of Malabar in 1915, there were 86 land-owning families who paid one-fifth of the entire land revenue of Malabar, while they owned thousands of acres of land. Most of them were high caste Hindus and only two of them were Moplahs. Similarly, according to a study made in 1881-82, of the 829 prominent land-owners, 370 Namboothris, 379 Nairs, 61 Rajas, 93 Non-Malayali Brahmins, eight Tiyas, four other Hindus, one was a European and 37 were Moplahs. In the Taluks of Ernad and Walluvanad which were the worst affected during the Moplah revolt, the situation was worse. Of 292 large land-owners, 173 were Namboothiris, 96 were Nairs, 20 Rajas and only three Moplahs. To justify the inequitable land distribution, the Namboothiris had fabricated an interesting *parante* explanation. According to this, Lord

Parashurama had acquired this land from the Ocean for their enjoyment.

This kind of land distribution, which left 95 per cent of the population landless, gave birth to an inhuman agrarian relationship. Contemporary literature and accounts are replete with the atrocities perpetuated by the Namboothir. In his '*Kerala-Yesterday, Today and Tomorrow*", the Marxist author, E.M.S. Namboothiripad, himself—a Namboothiris, has given a detailed and vivid portrait of the world based on the inhuman social organisation created by the Namboothiri Brahmins. The Moplahs and other Hindus suffered similar oppression at the hands of the landlords, especially the Namboothiris. The difference was that like their fellow lower-caste brethren in other parts of the country, the exploited Hindus accepted their bestial conditions of life as their fate whereas the Muslims had no such compulsions. Although their origins were in the lower castes of Hindu society, after their conversion to Islam, they came under the influence of a worldview that preaches equality to all.

Apart from the oppression of the landlords, the entry of religious zeal into their lives was a source of encouragement for the Moplahs in their continuous struggle. One example will suffice to explain the ridiculous length to which religion influenced their lives. During the First World War, the Moplahs came to believe that Germany had accepted Islam and, with the entry of Turkey on its side, the defeat of the British and their allies had become inevitable. The Moplahs had no doubt of the victory of what they considered to be Islamic forces, *i.e.*, Germany and Turkey, against the forces of Christianity represented by the British and their allies. This is the reason that for them the *Khilafat* movement was more a battle for their faith than an anti-imperialistic struggle. Even in their earlier struggles between 1886-1919, the use of religious symbols can be seen. Usually, the participation in a struggle was seen as a sacrifice for their religion by the Moplahs. A Moplah was well aware of the fact that resistance to the land system protected and strengthened by the might of the Raj was bound to end in failure and so, before leaving for any struggle he donned the white clothes of a martyr, divorced his wives, sought the forgiveness of his neighbours for any fault he may have been guilty of, and asked for the blessings of his religious leaders. Religious frenzy filled these participants with a strange suicidal urge.[31] That is the reason that why each struggle reproduced the same sequence of events. After killing some Hindus, the Moplahs would gather in a mosque or some other religious building to await the arrival of the British forces. They preferred fighting to being taken alive. Between 1836 and 1919 there were 29 occasions when the Moplahs invited death in this fatal fashion.

As a result of their religious frenzy, the Moplahs often killed Hindus other than money-lenders, who were themselves from the lower castes and suffered from oppression similar to their own. In the 29 incidents mentioned above, 82 Hindus were killed. The castes of 78 have been established—63 were upper castes (23 Namboothiri Brahmins, six non-Malayali Brahmins, 34 Nairs and others, while 15 belonged to the Shudra lower castes).

After the take-over of Malabar by the East India Company in 1792, land relations became more anti-Moplah. The British officers of the Madras Presidency and Malabar accepted the fact that as compared to the landless, the landholder upper caste Hindus were more useful to them and strengthening them contributed to the stability of the Raj. While there were a few British officers who advocated land reforms and tried to protect the Moplahs from eviction, they were always in a minority. The East India Company and later on the Imperial British Government always made laws that strengthened the land-owners and worsened the conditions of the Moplahs. In particular, the landlords were given the right to evict tenants and also to occupy grazing lands that were not owned by any particular individual, with ease.

For the Moplahs, the British and the Jenmis or landlords were equally their enemies. While one looted them, the other crushed their resistance. The Moplahs' hearts were filled with hatred and revolt for both their oppressors and they gave vent to their feelings through sporadic violent clashes that they indulged in from time to time. It was these emotions that were translated into support for the Congress movement of *Khilafat* and non-cooperation.

The Congress presence was felt very late in Malabar. It held its first district conference in Palghat in May 1916. If we analyse the class character of those who participated in the conference, we will find that it was dominated by the very people whom the Moplahs regarded as their traditional enemies. We have definite information regarding the professions of 358 delegates, 27 per cent of them were landlords and their agents, 33 per cent were lawyers and the rest were middle class professionals like traders, money-lenders, industrialists, tea- and coffee-planters, clerks, teachers, doctors and journalists. The Moplahs could not identify with any of these categories. There were only two Moplah delegates and both of them were prosperous land-owners.

The class character of the Congress delegates helps us to understand the way in which its programmes were formalised and also the Moplah reaction to these programmes. It would be meaningless to expect landlords and their supporters to include land reforms on their agenda. It would also be unfair to expect the Moplahs to extend their support to programmes initiated by landlords or lawyers who were their greatest enemies in their struggle against eviction in the courts or those middle class professionals who were completely indifferent to their misery. They participated whole-heartedly in the non-cooperation and *Khilafat* movements because they perceived them as a means of expressing their anger against the British, whom they considered as being largely responsible for their sufferings and also as a means of their participation in a holy war against the British who had defeated the Turks and destroyed the supremacy of the *Khilafat*.

From the very inception of the *Khilafat* and non-cooperation programmes, it became obvious that Congress would not succeed in its objective of making the Moplahs fight against one enemy, the British, while maintaining friendly relations with the other enemy, the landlords. The atmosphere of religious frenzy that the average Moplah was surrounded by was a decisive factor in determining the direction of Moplah action. This is why Moplah behaviour towards the Hindus was marked by cruelty and intolerance from the very beginning. The illusions of the Congress leaders, who believed that the *Khilafat* movement by itself could bring about Hindu-Muslim unity, were destroyed very early. The movement proved to be more disastrous for the Hindus than the British. When the first Moplah Raj was proclaimed in Pokkotur, those issuing the proclamation made it very clear that all non-believers (Kafirs) would face death in Moplah Raj.

In the course of the movement, the Hindus were offered choice between death and conversion. The fragile nature of Hindu-Muslim unity is best illustrated in an excerpt from a notice issued by the secretary, *Khilafat* Committee of Tanur, Anummanakath Parikutti. The Moplah understanding of Swaraj and non-cooperation is stated as "the bounden duty of all Muslims to endeavour in attaining Swaraj for all Muslims and to non-cooperate with the other religionists who are enemies of our religion."

The Moplah revolt was actually a symbol of the failure of the well-intentioned belief of the Congress leaders that they could forge lasting and meaningful unity between the Hindus and the Muslims merely by asking the Hindus to participate in the *Khilafat* movement and the Muslims in movements like Cow Protection. This belief ignored the fact that the *Khilafat* movement was a narrow, fundamentalist movement which would result almost everywhere in increased Muslim communal consciousness and embittered relations between the Hindus and the Muslims. Even if good relations between the two communities were exhibited in a few places, these were always superficial and short-lived. The progressive Muslim leadership stayed away from this movement and it is no accident that it was given its final burial by the progressive Muslim leadership of Turkey itself. If those who were encouraging the Moplahs to join the *Khilafat* and non-cooperation movement really felt that they would establish Hindu-Muslim unity in this way, then they were living in an unreal and imaginary world. This is borne out by the results of these movements. Had the Congress made land reforms an important part of their programme instead of *Khilafat* and united the Moplahs with the vast majority of the lower caste exploited Hindu peasantry in a struggle against landlords, the result would perhaps have been different. It would be an over-simplification to say that a struggle for an economic cause would have easily removed the religious frenzy from the lives of Moplahs. But, it can definitely be said that only a united struggle for land reforms could have resulted in lasting Hindu-Muslim unity in Malabar. Such a struggle could have, in due course, encouraged a real anti-imperialist struggle that would have converged with the national movement. Seeing the class character of the Congress leadership, however, it would be expecting too much from them to mobilise the landless Moplahs against the Jenmis and the landlords.

The Bengal Riots : In the early part of the 20th century, Hindu-Muslim conflict became endemic in Bengal especially East Bengal. These conflicts were caused by land issues similar to those in Malabar and by the communal rigidity continuously developed by various religious and cultural movements. The conflicts of Bengal help to illustrate the fact that fundamentalist leaders who are usually sympathisers of the wealthy sections and work to protect their interests, use religious symbols to incite communal frenzy among the weaker sections of society. All the communal riots of the early 20th century in Bengal are actually attempts through communal expressions to obtain solutions for socio-economic problems.

Between 1906 and 1946, the major communal riots that occurred in Bengal were as follows—1906-07 in Mymensing, 1918-1926 in Calcutta, Pabna and Dhaka, 1930 in Kishoreganj, 1931 in Chittagong, 1941 in Dhaka and 1946 in Calcutta. One factor common to all these riots was the emphasis placed by the Mullahs on the religious aspect of the exploitation of the poor Muslims by the Hindu landlords and money-lenders and their insistence on Islam as the means of their economic salvation. This is the reason why during most communal rioting, Muslim mobs made Hindu landlords and money-lenders in the villages and Marwari traders in the towns, responsible for high prices and hoarding and made them targets of their violence. While weaker groups of the Hindus like milkmen, washermen, sweepers and fishermen often got caught up in communal violence—this was usually the exception in earlier riots. This situation changed in the later riots of 1930-46 when the riots were perceived as an effective means for the establishment of a separate Muslim state. During these riots, mob attacks on all the Hindus became part of the overall religious and political design.

Religious leaders used great ingenuity to hide the fact from their followers that only a small percentage of the

Hindus were money-lenders or landlords. According to one description of Mymensing, half of the Rs. 80 lakhs of revenue collected was distributed among 25 persons belonging to the Saha, Nawashakh and Banik castes.[32] Similarly, the Marwari and Saha—moneylenders charged from 25 to 50 per cent interest and some time this went up to 100 per cent. It was not only Muslims who were the victims of this loot and exploitation, a large proportion of the Hindu population suffered in equal measure. The Hindu rayots like their Muslim counterparts, paid several taxes to the landlord in addition to the land rent. These included gifts to the landlords and their officers, the landlords payer tax and taxes that ranged from a tax when a new class was opened in a school or tax that was paid for a wedding in the landlord family or a tax to be paid on his birthday. Without making an offering to the landlord, a peasant could not dig a pond or build a house or cut a tree. No landlord ever gave the peasant a title deed of the land. The only proof he had of his right to the land was a receipt for the land revenue that he paid and this receipt was very ambiguous. The landlords had unlimited powers of eviction which they utilised mercilessly. But, all these facts were as real for the Hindus as they were for the Muslims. The Hindus suffered as much at the landlords' hands as did the Muslims. Similarly, there is not a single example of a money-lender charging less interest from a Hindu than from a Muslim. Nor did he resort to less cruel methods in collecting his dues in either case. While there were, few Muslim landlords, there is no example of their treating their Muslim tenants with any kindness. They were as cruel as their Hindu counterparts. Given the conditions of lack of education (according to 1911 census, 4.14 per cent and according to 1931 census 5.69 per cent of the Muslims were literate) and the lack of a secular symbol, it was only natural that the Bengali Muslims easily fell prey to the propaganda of their mullahs that the Hindus were responsible for their misery and exploitation. This is why they gave expression to their desire for liberation from misery and exploitation by attacking visible symbols of exploitation during riots. A unique feature of the riots of Mymensing (1906-1907), Calcutta (1918-1926), Pabna (1926) and Dhaka (1926) was the looting of the money-lenders' accounts books and the landlords' records of land pledged to them. The humiliation inflicted upon the Marwaris in the cities and attacks on them were also expressions of this anger. In the earlier riots, only those temples were attacked for whose upkeep the landlords extorted taxes from the rayots. It would be over-simplification to identify these struggles as class struggles. In fact, mullahs reduced the economic content of protest (anti-exploitation) and converted it into a struggle of fanaticism (anti-Hindu). Religious fanatics kept trying to give these struggles a religious colour and, as a result, the poor classes were often at the receiving end of the distortion introduced by the riots. After 1930, the suffering inflicted on these classes increased because by then the political significance of rioting had been realised and it was easy enough to bring these poor people on the streets and use them for swelling the violent crowds.

This example is enough to understand how economic issues were utilised in a communal fashion in riots in Bengal. The mullahs advocated that their poor co-religionists should pray five times a day, refuse to accept food from the Hindus and not give any donations to Hindu rituals as part of their obligations as tenants. They also propagated that Muslims should not work as domestic servants in Hindu homes and that Muslim prostitutes should not cater to Hindu clients.[33] These mullahs had no objection to the institution of prostitution nor did they ever demand that Muslim prostitutes should not sell themselves to Muslims. During Mymensing riots, certain prostitutes who were kept by Hindu landlords were attacked, their property was looted and they were forced into marriage with Muslims. Similarly, Muslim servants who hesitated to leave their Hindu masters were attacked.

The opportunistic use made of economic issues by communal politicians is illustrated by another example, that of the stand of Muslim League to land reform bills in the Bengal Legislative Assembly. The Muslim League which in the United Provinces represented big landlords and Zamindars and opposed landreform programmes, stood for landreforms in Bengal. The Krishak Praja Party which largely represented Muslim interests, was also a supporter of land reforms. Congressmen opposed any attempt at land reforms, as active spokesmen of the landlords in the legislative assembly. The Muslim League and the Krishak Praja Party tried their utmost to reduce the rates of interest charged by moneylenders, while the Congress whole-heartedly opposed this. Muslim newspapers advocated the cause of the poor classes while the Hindu newspapers always wrote in favour of the landlords and moneylenders. The reasons are very clear. The Congress and Hindu press opposed land reforms and all attempts to control usury only because they felt that these were anti-Hindu measures. On the other hand, Muslim political parties and newspapers felt that advocating the cause of the poorer sections was their religious duty because Muslims in Bengal stood on the lowest rung of the economy.

The Cow Protection Movement: The Cow Protection Movement of the late 19th century and early 20th century and the terrible riots it engendered in Mumbai, Bihar and Eastern UP were manipulated through the use of religious symbols to serve social, economic and political purposes. While the Mumbai riots were restricted to industrial settlements, the riots in Bihar and Eastern UP covered large rural areas. The riots that affected thousands of square miles in Azamgarh, Ballia, Ghazipur, Saran, Shahibabad, Gaya and Patna severely affected the working of the law and order machinery for several years. According to the memoirs of some English bureaucrats, after 1857-58 this was the greatest turmoil in the Bhojpuri-speaking area.

The first organised and armed attempt at cow protection came to be seen in the Kuka revolt, but this remained a limited and localised movement. It was the Arya Samaj that brought the movement to the national level and made it a symbol of Hindu honour. With the expansion of the Arya Samaj, Goraksha Samitis sprang up all over the country. In 1885, the Goraksha Mandali was formed in Delhi and in November 1889, Bal Gangadhar Tilak became its leading light in Pune. According to the Governor of Mumbai Presidency, Harris, the rioting that broke out on August 11, 1893, in Mumbai was the result of the communal frenzy spread by the Cow Protection Mandali.

The movement against cow slaughter that spread all over Eastern UP after 1887-88 had its origin in a decision of the Allahabad Municipal Board to change its by-laws in order to ban cow slaughter and the refusal of the Allahabad High Court to uphold this decision to give legal sanction to a religious belief. As a result, Cow Protection Societies sprang up in many towns. With astounding speed and extraordinary organisational ability, the movement spread to remote rural areas in Bhojpuri-speaking Eastern UP and Bihar and, as a result, the lives and property of Muslims on a very large scale were destroyed in these areas.

It was not just a desire to protect the cow that motivated the Cow Protection Movement. Very often strong vested interests were found behind it. It must be remembered that the leadership of the movement was usually in the hands of feudal elements. The landlords of the Bhojpuri-speaking areas of Eastern UP and Bihar were mostly Bhumihars, Kshatriyas and Brahmins and these castes played a dominant role in the movement. The Raja of Darbhanga and his relative, Lal Chhatrapati Singh or Loshi Upadhyay, are examples of the feudal leadership.[34]

Two very interesting facts emerge from a study of the movement that throw light on the extra-religious motives of the forces behind it. Many incidents occurred of the landlords attempting to evict Muslim tenants from their land after accusing them of slaughtering cows. It was obviously an attempt on the part of the Hindu landlords to find a pretext to evict their troublesome Muslim tenants. Very often the refusal of the Muslim tenant to pay increased land tax or his reluctance to pay the arrears, led to the charge of cow slaughter against him. In many cases, economic rivalries between the Hindu and the Muslim landlords led to the use of the pretext of the Muslim landlords encouraging cow slaughter. In all these cases the common *modus operandi* used to be the instigating of a Hindu mob by Hindu landlord, against his Muslim tenant or a rival Muslim landlord, by accusing him of slaughtering cows.

On the other hand, attempts by lower-castes Hindus to improve their social standing by way of participating in a 'religious act' also came to the fore. Especially members of the Koeri, Ahir and Kurmi castes started wearing the sacred thread, affixing surnames like Singh and Rai and participating enthusiastically in this 'Holy' act in order to improve their status within the caste-ridden Hindu social structure. An amusing point is that this effort on their part was resisted by the upper castes among both Hindu and Muslim landlords in Muzaffarpur, Patna and Darbhanga. On many occasions members of the backward castes had to face active opposition and oppression from both. It is interesting that the people striving for equality and self-respect could be utilised for a communal cause but would not be granted equality by those who were utilising them.

REFERENCES

1. Prof. Bipin Chandra, *Communalism in Modern India*, p. 22.
2. Ramanandi, *Vaishnav Sanyasis.*
3. Neville, *District Gazetteer of Barabanki*, p. 169.
4. Wife of Nawab Shuja-ud-daulah and the mother of Nawab Asaf-ud-daulah did not leave Faizabad at the time of the shifting of the capital of Avadh to Lucknow. In 1816, she entered into an agreement with the East India Company according to which Faizabad and Avadh came under the influence of the Company for the purposes of revenue collection and policing.
5. Neville, *District Gazetteer of Barabanki*, p. 170.
6. Tarachand, *History of Freedom Movement in India*, pp. 485-486.
7. *Times of Indian Year Book*,1923.
8. *The District Gazetteer of Banaras (1907)*, pp. 207-8.
9. Mohd. Yasin, *A Social History of Islamic India* (1958).
10. *Kalhana-Rajatarangini*,Trans. by Ranjit Sita Ram Pandit, p. 352.
11. Gyanendra Pandey, *The Construction of Communalism in Colonial North India*, p. 16.
12. Nalinaksh Sanyal, *Development of Indian Railways (1930).*
13. Henry Mead, *The Sepoy Revolt*, pp. 126-127.
14. *Travels in Asia and Africa*, pp. 233-34. Trans. of Ibn Batuta's travel experiences by H.A.R. Gibb.
15. Elliot & Dowson, *The History of India*, Vol. VIII, p. 48.
16. Neville, *District Gazetteer of Faizabad* (1905), pp. 173-174.
17. Prof. R.S. Sharma, *Communal History and Rama's Ayodhya.*
18. Peter van der Veer, "God must be liberated. A Hindu liberation movement in Ayodhya", *Modern Asian Studies*. Vol. 21, No. 2, p. 287.

19. W.E. Benet, *Gazetteer of Lucknow* (1877), p. 7.
20. Peter van der Veer, 'God must be Liberated'.
21. *Ibid.*, Michael Fisher, *A Clash of two cultures : Avadh, the British and the Moghuls,* pp. 228-236 and J.R.I. Cole-Roots, *North Indian Shiism: Religion and State in Avadh,* 1772-1859, pp. 244-49.
22. During my visit to Ayodhya, a very interesting anecdote by an old man was narrated to me which he claimed to have heard from his grandfather who was a witness to the British repression after the revolt of 1857. According to this anecdote, Nawab Wajid Ali Shah hanged the leaders of Hindu and Muslim warring factions who fought on the issue of Babri Mosque -Ramjanambhoomi in 1853-1855 on a *neem* tree. Later on the elders of both the communities entered into an agreement and the dispute almost ended. After suppressing the revolt of 1857, Britishers hanged the leaders of the two communities who were instrumental in achieving a peaceful solution on the same *neem* tree. There is no historical evidence in favour of this anecdote but it emphasises the understanding of the common people regarding policies of the British Imperialism.
23. J.F. Sale, *National Archives,* New Delhi.
24. E.M., Rogers, *National Archives,* New Delhi.
25. N.G. Barrier, Statement of Radhey Raman Aggarwal, *Roots of Communal Politics,* p. 280.
26. Statement of Munshi Noor llahi before Congress Commission, p. 290.
27. Statement of Abdul Haq before Congress Commission, p. 290.
28. N.S. Saxena, *Communal Riots in India,* p. 13.
29. G.I. Boag, *Census of India,* 1921 Vol. xiii, Part-2, pp. 118-123.
30. Conard Wood, *The Moplah rebellion and its Genesis,* p. 17.

31. Sir Percival Griffith, *To Guard my people: The History of the Indian Police*, p. 287.
32. Suranjan Dass, *Communal riots in Bengal*, 1905-1947.
33. S. Sarkar, *Swadeshi Movement in Bengal*, 1903-8.
34. Gyanendra Pandey, *The Construction of Communalism in Colonial North India*, p. 192.

3

The Psycho-social Dimensions of Communal Riots

In order to give legitimacy to any communal violence, every community advances its own arguments. These arguments take such deep root in the thought process of individual members of each community that they begin to think of them as part of their cultural identity. Based on these arguments, a community builds prejudices against other communities, considering themselves as peaceful, tolerant, generous and pious and treating members of other communities as naturally violent, cunning, fanatic and Independable. These are the kinds of prejudices that a community nurtures and is not prepared to brook any arguments against. Even when the behaviour of a community has been totally indefensible, an attempt is made to justify the same by faulting the attitude of the other community[1] to deflect criticism of its own misdemeanour. It is not only communal forces that exaggerate the cruelty of the other community in order to provoke their own community to violence but even the relatively liberal intellectual class tries to justify the violent acts of its own community.[2] Too often, the innocence and non-violent character of one's own community is supported by arguments in such an indecorous seriousness that to accept these arguments would mean the negation of logical behaviour and all human frailty. These arguments are used to prove that one community remains always peaceful and law-abiding and its violence is only a reaction in self-defence to the violence of the other community.[3]

In the Indian context, this attempt can be witnessed in the big movements organised by Muslim and Hindu communalists. The Muslim League was successful in conveying the message to a vast number of Muslims that the Hindus and the Muslims constitute different nations. That the Muslims of the Indian sub-continent despite their varied differences in cultural traditions, languages, food habits and apparel and despite the geographical distances between them, are one nation because they shared a common religion, Islam. This distortion of reality preached by the Muslim League was not only believed by the large number of Muslims but they actually fought for the establishment of a Muslim Nation.[4] How hollow this misconception that based nationality on religion was, became apparent when the Muslim area of East Pakistan emerged as a separate nation in 1971.

Similarly, the forces of *Hindutva* have been raising the question of a 'national mainstream' over the last few decades. These forces want Indian Muslims to merge with the national mainstream. But, what is this national mainstream? These forces have no concrete answer to this question. If the mainstream is a Hindu mainstream, then which Hindu mainstream is it? The Brahmin mainstream or the Shudra mainstream or the Bengali Hindu mainstream or the Punjabi Hindu mainstream? All the contradictions that can possibly exist in a pluralistic society are to be found in Hindu and Indian society. Very often these contradictions are based on points of conflict rather than just on disagreement. The slogan of the *Hindutva* forces that 'those who speak in the interest of the Hindus, will rule the country'[5] attempt to make Hindus accept the distortion, that because they are Hindus they have a common interest (which is opposed to the interests of those belonging to the other religions) and, therefore, they should vote together (to ultimately bring a Hindu *Rashtra* into being).

The psychology of violence has its own logic. However this logic changes with the times. During the medieval period, religion intervened in people's lives more decisively and so the violence of this period was justified with the use of religious symbolism. The crusades or *'Jehads'* fought between the Muslims and the Christians or the Brahmin-Buddhist and Shaivite-Vaishnavite conflicts are examples of religious violence. Destruction of the places of worship of the 'enemy' as well as forced conversions were the important aspects of this violence. A sense of religious duty was often behind this violence. Participants in the violence were convinced that they would attain heaven if they were killed in the course on this earth. The question of identity and security was not as crucial in the feudal system as it became when times changed and the era of capitalistic development of the means of production dawned. The changes that have occurred in productive relations have changed the internal balance of society to such an extent that religion as such cannot be presented as the only panacea for all human problems. The more developed human consciousness that has been created by the constant interaction between science and different ideologies, will no longer grant social sanction to the kind of religious wars that were fought in the medieval period. This is why even one of the groups organised in the name of religion in the contemporary world, Pan Islamism, which is quite a strong force, is unable to enthuse its enormous following for *'Jehad'* with the slogan of 'Islam in danger' in Afghanistan, Kashmir or Bosnia-Herzegovina. It has not been able to mobilise any Islamic country or people to the extent that any one of these issues would have done in medieval times.

In the contemporary world, violence has to find a material justification rather than a purely religious one. While these justifications have some religious ramifications, these are basically materialistic. Two sources have contributed most towards disturbing the equilibrium created between social relationships that have existed for many years. These are the changes in, production and democracy. Capitalist methods of production have not only brought about changes like the development of cities, the creation of modern and fast modes of transportation, universalisation of education, equality of the sexes *etc.*, but have also given birth to the concepts of imperialism, colonialism, wars and social systems based on exploitation and inequality. Naturally, these changes have created tensions that the world had not known earlier. It is now difficult for the elite sections to make the vast numbers of the deprived, exploited and miserable people believe that the reasons for their sorrows are other-worldly. People are now looking for material causes and solutions for their problems rather than being satisfied with other-worldly ones like divine intervention, fate, re-birth, heaven and hell.

As an institution, democracy has also challenged the assertion of those who claim divine sanction for social inequality and their efforts to justify it. This challenge of democracy has naturally turned the equilibrium of social relationships topsy-turvy. Actually, communalism is the most effective intervention on the part of the ruling classes to maintain their supremacy in the contemporary world. By the use of the weapon of communalism, the ruling classes place certain 'solutions' of their worldly problems before the oppressed people in such a cunning way that instead of organising themselves against their oppressors, they fight amongst themselves.

Tension based on material factors developed more sharply in Indian society after the arrival of the Britishers. This kind of tension was quite different from the religious tensions that existed between the Hindus and the Muslims during the Muslim rule. These new tensions were national during the transition of the century from a feudal society based on agriculture and handicrafts to an industrial capitalist society. The hostility of the Muslims towards western education made them very backward as far as employment opportunities were concerned. It was also obvious that if an election based on universal suffrage was held, then their share in government would be proportionately less than that of the Hindus. The Mullah-Landlord Muslim leadership took advantage of this fact to convince a large number of Muslims that the only solution to their problems lay in the preservation of their separate identity.

It is not an accident that feudal elements were the leaders of both Hindu and Muslim communal forces. The leadership of the Muslim League and the Hindu Mahasabha were in the hands of the upper castes and big landlords. These elements actively used communalism to promote their class interests. Riots were the most effective weapon that they never hesitated to use, in order to prevent unity of the working classes of the Hindus and the Muslims.

There is no single cause for the continuance of communal rioting after independence in both Pakistan and India. In order to understand the phenomenon, the character of the modern Indian state, the kind of economic development taking place in the country and the effects of these on various social groups and institutions will have to be studied. In addition, we have to take into account the factors like the behaviour of political parties during elections, the use of communal propaganda and polarisation to increase their spheres of influence, distribution of tickets by political parties on communal and caste basis, the emergence of organised crime, large scale unemployment, and the competition for jobs that this unemployment generates. These and other related factors emerge as causes whenever riots occur. In recent years, it is the Hindu middle class that has become the most communalised. Its antipathy towards the pro-backward and scheduled caste rhetoric of important political parties is also responsible for making it a supporter of the

Hindutva movement. The well-organised movement for the construction of the Ram Mandir by the *Hindutva* forces is the main result of this development. The state could not mount an effective opposition to this movement. After independence, the greatest communalisation of the Hindus and the most terrible riots can be attributed to this single movement. It is due to this movement that dozens of towns, cities and villages that had no previous history of rioting of even during the worst days of partition, witnessed riots.

Who Initiates Riots : The Myth and the Reality

The attitude of the majority community or the Hindus towards riots is based on two pre-determined beliefs. They are convinced that it is the Muslims who start the riots and it is the Hindus who suffer more in the course of rioting. Behind these pre-determined beliefs are certain formulations that are deeply rooted in the Hindu psyche. The average Hindu is convinced that the Hindus are by nature liberal, spiritual, tolerant and non-violent. As opposed to this, Muslims are by nature cruel, violent, treacherous and fanatic. Once both these formulations have become a part of the Hindu psychology, it is not difficult for a large number of the Hindus also to believe, that it is the Muslims who start riots and that mostly the Hindus suffer due to these riots. It is only natural to assume that a 'cruel and fanatic' community will start riots and that a non-violent and tolerant community will be most harmed.

In order to understand the psychology of communal riots in India it is interesting to go into a detailed study of both the formulations-so strongly believed by the Hindus.

Usually the question of who starts the riots—the Muslims or the Hindus—can be a debatable point because the same fact can be discussed in many and, sometimes, contradictory ways. While there is a scope for debate on the starting of a riot there can be none as far as the number of those killed. It is better, therefore, to first examine the belief held by the Hindus about those who are killed during riots. Even if only government figures are believed upon and the figures supplied by various Muslim organisations are dismissed as exaggerations, not only are those killed in riots predominantly Muslims but more than 60 per cent of those killed in more than half of the riots that have occurred after Independence are Muslims. While Government statistics in India are often viewed with suspicion, it is well-known that no government in the world would easily publish such facts which show that minorities are not secure in its country. Hence, it may be safe to believe the statistics provided by the government.

A glance at the chart given below is sufficient to demonstrate the extent of the misconception harboured by the Hindus regarding the religion of those killed in riots.

Year	**No. of Incidents**	**Killed**		**Total**
		Hindus	**Mulims**	
1968	346	24	99	133
1969	519	66	558	674
1970	512	68	176	298
1971	312	38	65	103
1972	210	21	45	70
1973	242	26	45	72
1974	248	26	61	87
1975	205	11	22	33
1976	169	20	19	39
1977	188	12	24	36
1978	219	51	56	108
1979	304	80	150	216
1980	427	87	278	375
Total	**3949**	**530**	**1598**	**2289**

Source: Law and Order: Reading and Cases; Published by Lal Bahadur Shastri National Academy of Administration, Mussoorie.

These statistics are included in the reports by the Union Ministry of Home Affairs from time to time. The total number of those killed exceed the number of the Hindus and the Muslims killed because it includes police personnel, people belonging to other communities and also those who have not been identified.

It would also be relevant to have a look at figures of Hindus and Muslims killed in some major riots during the last few years:

Name of Place	Number of People Killed			
	Hindu	**Muslims**	**Other & Unidentified**	**Total**
Aligarh (1961)	1	12	13	
Ranchi/Hatia (August, 1967)	20	156	1	177
Ahmedabad (Sept., 1969)	24	430	58	512
Bhiwandi (May, 1970)	17	59	2	78
Jalgaon (May, 1970)	1	42	-	43
Firozabad (1972)	3	16	2	21
Aligarh (1979)	6	19	3	28
Moradabad (Aug. Sept, 80)	18	142	0	166
Meerut (1982) (Upto 3rd Oct. 1992)	6	21	2	29
Total	**96**	**897**	**74**	**1066**

Both the lists given above make it amply clear that in the riots after independence except for some minor exceptions, not just more Muslims but many more Muslims than Hindus have been killed.

Further, police action during and after riots is also concentrated against the Muslims. In the next chapter we will see that even in those riots during which only the Muslims were killed, those arrested were also mostly

Muslims, the homes searched were mostly those of the Muslims and the torture of curfew had also to be endured by them. These are not secret facts. The secular and Urdu press especially, publish reports after every riot that describe the unjust treatment meted out to the Muslims. While such reports are often exaggerated, the message that they send out clearly to the Muslims is that if riots occur, they will be the main people to be killed, their houses will be searched and they will be arrested. If even after this, it is believed that Muslims start riots then the reasons for holding this belief will have to be examined because it suffers from logical inconsistencies. No community, unless it is motivated by an urge to commit mass suicide or self destruction or unless it has gone completely mad, will start a riot when it is convinced that it is going to suffer the consequences most. We will have to examine minutely the point of time when a riot is supposed to have started, to appreciate this notion better.

Flash Point in the build-up towards Communal Violence

If we study the violence in a riot from a sociological point of view, we will find that this violence develops like a pyramid. The urge to violence already exists in the many facets of tension and conflict present in the social make-up. The preparation for large scale communal violence starts much earlier than its actual occurrence. The tension flowing through many stages of conflict comes to a flash point where a stray brickbat or rumour is enough to trigger off violence. The reasons behind this pyramid of tension building up and then erupting into violence over a relatively minor irritant can be many. The commercial rivalry between the Hindu and the Muslim traders, the interest in a piece of land or building by land mafias, and elections are some of the causes which can be utilised by an influential group to constantly misuse points of tension and to keep an area volatile that the smallest incident can result in large scale violence. Very often, there is no correlation between the immediate cause and general atmosphere of tension. It could be, for example, that the main reason for the tension in an area is a particular place of worship but the violence starts after two cyclists—one a Hindu and the other a Muslim—collide with each other. A small incident like this can only result in violence if tension already exists like a sufficient quantity of gun-power, waiting to be ignited. That is why similar incidents cause different reactions in different areas. For example, a communal riot does not occur every time two cyclists—a Hindu and a Muslim collide with each other.

Justice D.P. Madon in the course of his enquiry into the Bhiwandi-Jalgaon riots of 1970 gives a very convincing interpretation of the theories about how a riot starts. "If we were to take a surface view of the bare facts of any riot, it would appear that the riot was caused by an incident so insignificant, that we would be amused about how such a trifling matter, could have led to so much arson, looting and murder. It, however, does not require any deep insight to know that this incident was not the real cause of the riot but was merely the result of something else, which concretely expressed itself in the riot."

It would be relevant to study the process for the development of tension and the throwing of the first brickbat and the relationship between the two by looking at the sequence of events during some of the riots since independence.

The Ranchi Riot of 1967

On the 22nd of August, 1967, a riot began in Ranchi at 3.30 pm. The apparent reason for rioting was very simple. A procession of Hindu boys protesting against the 'imposition' of Urdu was stoned by some Muslims. The rioting began. If we look at the events of 10 days preceding the 22nd of August, the slogans raised by the processionists and what they did after the procession dispersed, only then the correct picture emerges.

In 1967, a United Legislators Front Government came to power in Bihar which included the Jan Sangh as one of its constituents. This front which comprisedalmost all of the non-Congress political parties, had issued a 33-point manifesto that included the promise to make Urdu the second official language of the state if the front was voted to power. The Jan Sangh which was part of the government was opposed to this. On the 14th July, 1967, when a non-official bill to make Urdu the second official language was moved in the State Legislature, the Jan Sangh, some members of the Congress and a non-official organisation—the Hindi Sahitya Sammelan, announced a state-wide agitation from the 12th to the 26th of August. An anti-Urdu fortnight was to be observed in Bihar during this period. In Ranchi, various anti-Urdu programmes were launched on the 12th of August. Prominent among these were the distribution of anti-Urdu leaflets and the taking out of processions with provocative slogans. The language of the leaflets was most offensive and objectionable. Arguments were put forward against Urdu and the Muslims. In a leaflett entitled "A challenge to the manhood of the new generation", the Muslims were declared anti-national, and the new generation, that is the students, were exhorted to stand up against them. On the 16th of August, a procession was taken out in the course of which minor skirmishes occurred. A look at the newspapers of the time reveals that the provocation increased in Ranchi day by day. Naturally as a defence mechanism, Muslims started taking measures to protect themselves. They were afraid that the processions which were being organised against Urdu might attack their persons and property.

This fear was justified by later events on the fateful day, when the procession was dispersed. Mayhem broke out all over the city between 22nd and 26th of August; as many as 184 people were killed, 164 of whom were Muslims. Such widespread violence could not have been caused merely by the brick-batting that the Muslims are said to have indulged in. Processions during the preceding ten days witnessed the processionists in the Central street, Hindpidi and Konka Road raising a provocative slogan, "If Urdu is forced on the boys, then blood will flow on the streets". The action of the stone-throwing Muslims was more the reaction of a frightened community that had been expecting to be attacked for the past ten days. On the 22nd of August, if they flung the first stone on the dispersing processionists whom they recognised as aggressors, then the point to be considered is whether this sole act constitutes the cause of the riot or whether the events of the earlier days and the deliberate political campaign that they were part of, and the tension that they had created are the real cause.

The Bhiwandi Riot of 1970

On May 7th, 1970, a communal riot erupted at Bhiwandi when a Shiva (Shivaji) Jayanti procession was attacked by a group of Muslims. This statement in one sentence conveys a simplistic explanation of the beginning of this riot but, if the events are looked at a little more closely, it becomes clear that it would not be desirable to jump to conclusions so easily. Tension did not start with Shiva Jayanti of that year but had been generated by the Shiva Jayanti celebrations of the previous years. The practice of the public observing Shiva Jayanti actually began in 1964. From the start, the way in which Shiva Jayanti was observed, introduced the poison of communalism in Bhiwandi. The organisers did not make any attempt to disguise the real motive, and anti-Muslim slogans and provocative floats were part of the celebrations from the very first year. In spite of the police opposition, the organisers made every attempt to incite rioting by insisting on taking their procession through the Muslim dominated areas, throwing coloured powder *(gulal)*, at mosques and shouting slogans like "we will grind any one who opposes us into dust". In report to his superiors, the Superintendent of Police, Thane, has clearly stated, "I found that a section of Hindu elements, particularly the R.S.S. and some P.S.P. men were bent upon creating mischief. Their idea in accompanying the procession was not so much to pay respects to the memory of the Great Shivaji but to establish their rights and if possible to provoke and humiliate Muslims."[6]

After the first big public demonstration in 1964, communal rioting was avoided during the Shiva Jayanti procession of 1965 and 1966. But on the 11th of May 1967, the first communal riot in the history of Bhiwandi did occur during the course of the Shiva Jayanti procession. According to the police records and the report of the Justice D.P. Madon Enquiry Commission, the rioting was the result of the irresponsible behaviour of the participants in the procession. By their acts of keeping the police in the dark about the timings and the route of the procession, their insistence on throwing coloured powder at the mosques and raising provocative slogans, despite police opposition, the processionists were successful in attaining their objective. The comment of Justice Madon clearly identifies the forces behind this attempt. "In 1967 municipal elections which took place thereafter (the skirmishes of 1967 Shiva Jayanti), so far as Hindu Councillors were concerned, all those who had taken an active part in this Shiva Jayanti Utsav were elected."[7] The 1967 riots submerged the entire life of Bhiwandi including the politics of the Municipal Board in the vicious atmosphere of communalism, whereas the years,1968 and 1969 were years of tension. During these years air of controversy hovered over the Shiva Jayanti processions but there were no riots. In such a scenario, it is more natural that between 1969 and 1970 tension would grip Bhiwandi over small incidents. Large scale rioting was averted over incidents like student programmes, the activities of the city Municipal Board and religious festivals. During this time, communal organisations of both Hindus and Muslims increased their strength in and around Bhiwandi and their leaders kept on spewing venom in the city.

The Shiva Jayanti procession of 7th May, 1970, was taken out in an atmosphere of mutual suspicion, hatred and tension. Communal Hindu organisations had been seen working on a campaign spreading malice around the towns and villages in the vicinity for several days. As a result, thousands of armed Hindus started pouring into Bhiwandi on the morning of the fateful day. The participants in the procession were not only equipped with kerosene oil and weapons like lathis, spears and choppers but also were exhibiting them openly. They were also shouting provocative and insulting slogans against the Muslims. Whenever the procession passed through a Muslim locality or in front of a mosque, their behaviour would become more provocative. In spite of being stopped by the police and the saner elements, they would throw colour powder in a way that it would fall on the mosques.

In the face of such provocation and apprehension, the Muslims must have also made arrangements for their security. While deposing before the Enquiry Commission, the Hindus and the Muslims gave conflicting versions about how the rioting started and which community made the first move. But even if we accept the fact that the Muslims threw the first stone at the procession, does that prove that Muslims started the Bhiwandi riots of 1970?

Very often, the way in which the first stone is thrown or the first hand is raised in aggression, suggests an outside agency at work, that wants to create a situation in which the members of the minority community commit an act that invites severe retribution for themselves. The outside agency could be a communal organisation or it could be a political party. This communal organisation does not necessarily have to be one ostensibly representing Hindu interests. The opinion of the international community, the existence of a free press in India, a dominating judiciary, adult suffrage that compels political parties to address themselves to the minorities, a modern and scientific educational system and the economic and social occasions that force the Hindus and the Muslims to interact on a large scale—these are the reasons why a strong community (the Hindus in the contemporary Indian context) will not like to be seen as physically attacking a weaker community (the Muslims in the same context). Any such initiative would not only render it vulnerable to outside hostility but would also injure its consciousness of looking itself as non-violent and liberal by nature. In order to guard against external criticism and to preserve their self-righteousness, the attack had to be seen as being made by the Muslims. It is as if the weaker person is pushed into a corner by the stronger one, forcing him to raise his hand so that he may be suitably punished for his 'attack'. Before the punishment is meted out, a suitable hue and cry can be made about the fact that because the person cornered is naturally wicked and violent, he is bound to attack first.

The riots of Jamshedpur (1979) and Banaras (1977) are two examples among the numerous ones of how a communalised situation is created in which Muslims are manoeuvred into apparently throwing the first stone. At both the places, the rioting started over the routes adopted by Hindu religious processions. A both the places, Hindu communalists insisted on routes that had not previously been used and which either passed through Muslim localities or in front of mosques. Moreover, the procession halted in the Muslim localities, and the armed and emotionally charged crowds of processionists indulged in provocative activities until the Muslims threw the first stone. No sooner had the first stone been thrown, then the violence of the majority community manifested its ugly face, only to damage Muslim lives and property on a large-scale . A detailed study of the two riots will enable us to appreciate this point better.

The Jamshedpur Riot of 1979

The riot that erupted in Jamshedpur in April 1979 was the result of the internal conflicts of the ruling Janata Party. The Karpoori Thakur (Janata Party) ministry included members of the erstwhile Jan Sangh that had merged itself in the Janata Party in 1977. The M.L.A. from Jamshedpur belonged to the Jan Sangh group and was known to be extremely communal. The *Ram Navami* procession of Jamshedpur had been taken out for years and its route was well established. In 1978, for the first time, taking the advantage of being the member of the ruling party, the local M.L.A. and various Hindu organizations brought pressure on the district administration to permit a deviation from the established route so as to take the procession and its accompanying 'Akharas' (groups of wrestlers usually armed with lathis and spears) along the route number 14. This route passed through Muslim localities and in front of a mosque of significant importance. Naturally, taking out a procession on such a route created tension. The tension gradually increased as the armed processionists began to shout provocative slogans. Somehow the administration succeeded in the procession peacefully. In the next year the organisers wanted to escorting use route number 14 for the procession, but this time the administration refused to permit any deviation from the traditional route. The controversy over the route of the procession was utilised by the Hindu organisations to communalise the atmosphere in the city. At the back of this controversy was the strong action taken by an honest and a strict Superintendent of Police against the Hindu and the Muslim mafias operating in Jamshedpur at that time. Both the mafias were interested in creating a communal problem to discredit and oust this officer from Jamshedpur. Subsequent analysis of the incidents proved that the underworld played a major role in the outbreak of the riot.

Those involved in taking out the procession on the 11th of April, 1979, made their intentions clear from the very beginning. While they announced that the time for the departure of the procession was 2 p.m., it started at 12 noon, sharp. Thousands of armed outsiders had been brought as participants. The processionists started shouting anti-Muslim slogans and before the police had a chance to stop them, the procession changed route and proceeded along the banned route number 14. Members of the *Akharas* participating in the procession, openly displayed their weapons like lathis, swords and spears. It was then that the critical incident occurred which will help us to understand the myth built up around the starting of a riot. The procession was halted in the midst of a densely populated Muslim locality, just as it came in front of an important mosque of the city. The leaders of the procession put forward some very illogical demands before the administration as a condition to move the procession further. The local M.L.A., and others started making provocative and fiery speeches to add to the atmosphere of tension. The processionists made menacing displays of weapons and shouted objectionable slogans for several hours. The efforts of the leadership to incite the processionists and at the same time the efforts of the administration to move them, continued for hours.

The spot where the procession halted was surrounded on all the four sides by Muslim houses. Finding themselves in the close vicinity of an armed frenzied mob bent on rioting, the Muslims also started collecting on their roofs with stones, boiling oil, lathis and spears. Many Muslims had collected in the mosque as well.

If we analyse the behaviour of the processionists, it becomes clear that they behaved like a group of people determined to provoke those whom they considered as their antagonists to cast the first stone. After several hours of trying, they finally achieved their objective. As darkness began to fall, the first stone was thrown from the mosque and the massacre started all over the city. The majority community had been successful in gaining the stamp of legitimacy for its own violence.

The Banaras Riot of 1977

What occurred in Banaras in 1977 was similar. Each year images of the Goddess Durga were taken to the Ganges for immersion in processions from various Bengali mohallas in the city. In the congested part of the city, these Bangali mohallas' neighbour were the densely populated Muslim localities.

The routes of the immersion processions were fixed. Just before the Durga Puja festival in 1977, communal friction between the Muslim weavers living near the Anglo-Bengali College and the Hindu neighbours had been created by incidents like the scaling of wall of the college by Muslim weaver boys, the use of college ground to spread yarn by Muslim weavers and playing of games by the college students. The Golden Sporting Club, a club of young Bengalees, demanded that it be allowed a new route for its Durga procession, a route that went through the narrow streets of Muslim mohallas. Obviously, this was a sinister demand made with an ulterior motive. The administration refused to accept it. On the 22nd of October, the administration had the procession taken out on the prescribed route and the immersion passed off peacefully.

This peaceful immersion did not satisfy those who had wanted to change the route of the procession. In the night, they placed a new idol where the old one had been and on the 23rd of October, they insisted in taking the new idol on the route for which permission had earlier been denied. The administration knowing fully well that this demand was totally unjustified, adopted a course of persuasion rather than dealing with them firmly as was required. The spot where this dispute took place, is the most congested and has mixed locality character in the city. Thousands of people collected during the arguments that lasted for several hours, while rumours spread through the city. The result of this dispute was what could be expected from such disputes. Communal Hindu leaders were able to convince the majority of Hindus in the city that the new idol was in fact the old one and that it could not be immersed because of the obstinacy of the Muslims.

The Muslims were apprehensive that if the Durga procession was taken through their localities, they would be attacked. The arguments that went on for hours in the street, the crowds that it collected and the resultant atmosphere of provocation—all created sufficient tension for a single stone to convert the situation into a riot. This stone did arrive from a Muslim roof and the rioting started.

These examples help us to understand that a riot does not really begin at the point when violence starts. The creation of tension starts much before this point is reached. In fact the tension builds up like a pyramid that gradually peaks at the point of violence. This point may be called the flash point in the build up towards communal violence. When the pyramid of tension has developed to its peak, any action by persons belonging to the two different religious groups, can lead to widespread communal rioting. When the pyramid does not exist, then very often, even a big communal incident can not spark off a riot. That is why the background of a riot should be examined before holding any community or person responsible for having started it. That which side has contributed more to the construction of the pyramid of tension must be properly ascertained.

When we investigate the question of how riots start, we should remember that the group responsible for starting a riot would have prepared for it in advance. The most important aspect of this preparation would be that of collection of arms. Because the Hindus are 'naturally non-violent', their religious processions are not believed to be armed and as such Muslims being violent by nature' would be better prepared. The behavioural pattern of the Muslims will make them attack first. It is also natural that whichever side attacks first will be in an advantageous position at least for some time. When we read newspaper accounts (mostly in the vernacular press) and police reports on rioting, the cause in most of the riots seems to be an attack by the Muslims on the Hindus. If this is to be accepted at face value, then, at least in the initial stage of the riot, the losses of the Hindus should be greater than of the Muslims, both in terms of person and property. (About the greater losses suffered by the Muslims in the rioting, the Hindus have their own explanation—after the Muslims have started the riot, the entry of the police, the armed police like PAC, BMP, SRP and the military, alters the situation and the losses the Muslims suffer are inflicted by these forces in their efforts to save the Hindus and control the riot. The underlying assumption is whatever losses the Muslims suffer, they bring upon themselves).

Two facts disprove the above assertions. In all the major riots, especially the ones that have occurred after independence, the Muslims have suffered from the very beginning of the riot. The kind of advantage that a well-prepared, 'cruel by nature' community intent on rioting should enjoy, has never accrued to them in any riot. It is worth remembering, that with the kind of resources that the police and riot-combating agencies have at their disposal, they are never in a position to intervene effectively in the riot for the first few hours.

Armed police like the PAC, BMP, SRP, para military forces like BSF and CRPF and the army are deployed to control riots after many hours, and, in some cases, after several days have elapsed. There is a long initial period, therefore, when the local police and administration transfer themselves from being helpless spectators into an effective force of intervention, when the two hostile communities have already had enough time to demonstrate their prowess. When we talk about the use of force by the police and the security forces, we must remember that their weapons are limited to a specific calibre. Those dying in riots are usually killed by stoning, arson, knifing or twelve-bore gun shots. Therefore, it would not be correct to say that the loss to the Muslims is inflicted only by the security forces. Very few are actually killed by them. The intervention of security forces helps the Hindu rioters in an altogether different way and that explains the soft approach they adopt towards them. This will be discussed in detail in the next chapter.

Mob: An Important Factor in Violence

The most important factor leading to a communal riot is the presence of an infuriated mob. The flesh point of departure of the pyramid of escalating provocation that we have talked about, the point at which violence starts, cannot be reached unless there is a frenzied mob present at that point. This mob has some basic characteristics. It is difficult to understand the behaviour of the mob and its contribution to the riot without understanding these characteristics.

In the context of communal rioting, we can call an anarchic group of a great number of individuals, a mob. The difference between a crowd and a mob can be gauged by the amount of anger present. While a crowd may often not display any anger at all, a mob does not become explosive without anger being present. Wherever the word 'crowd' is used in this study it refers to a 'mob'. It is not necessary that all the members of a mob are present at that particular place and time for the same reason. For example, a mob that is seized by religious frenzy may contain many individuals who are there for completely different reasons. One section of the crowd may be there either to take revenge for what it perceives as an insult to its religion or to teach a lesson to those belonging to another religion, another section may be interested in loot and yet another section may be looking forward to the effect that the rioting will have on the coming elections. In addition to these, there are any number of other reasons for the presence of members of the mob. The most interesting thing is that a very large number of its members may have actually no reason at all for their presence. There are many spots in a town or city where crowds collect either at different times of the day or night are is present throughout. Such spots may be near educational institutions, court premises, market places, district offices or are important cross roads of the area. Any sufficiently powerful nucleus will be able to draw the crowd already available at any of these places towards itself. In the Indian context, there are many significant examples of how an existing crowd could be used for communal mobilisation. During the Rama Janmabhoomi campaign, the *Hindutva* forces always gave the call for mobilisation in Ayodhya at a time when large number of pilgrims would have congregated there anyway. This served many purposes and provided the necessary crowd of persons already fired by religious zeal to be used for the communal mobilisation necessary for the success of the cause, with a minimum cost to the *Hindatva* forces themselves.

The second example is of areas inhabited predominantly by Muslims, where a large number of people are to be seen on the streets all day and night. The reason for this will be dealt with later, but the fact is, that in these areas also, a crowd can be collected without much effort. We can cite another example to underline the efforts of communal Muslim leadership to take advantage of the Muslim congregation assembled for some other purpose. It is a fact that calls by the Muslim leadership for collective action are normally given on Fridays when already a good number of Muslims are available in various mosques to respond to these calls. A valid example may be the call of the Muslim League of Bengal in undivided India to observe 'Direct Action Day' in 1946 on a Friday. The reason behind giving calls on Friday is not merely religious. It also highlights the desire of the Muslim leadership to use the congregation in religious places on Fridays for political purposes.

Very often the role of the leadership ends once it has collected a crowd and succeeded in arousing it to a frenzied pitch. It is very rare to find a chain of command remaining intact after the violence has begun. The leadership is marginalised by its own actions after collecting the crowd. The leaders start competing amongst themselves in order to increase their individual popularity. The crowd expresses its appreciation of various leaders with slogans and applause. In order to win acceptance from the crowd, the speakers try to outdo each other in their oratory. The more extreme the oratory, the greater the response from the crowd. Often a competition between the oratory and the response begins. The contradictions among the leaders also surface. Different elements within the leadership, in their efforts to evolve an enthusiastic response from the crowd, are caught in a crescendo of ever more provocative speeches. The vicious circle thus creatived by provocative speech—enthusiastic response—more provocative speech—leads the crowd to the point of hysteria and frenzy. This process gradually reduces the role of the leaders. Finally the frenzied mob either becomes leaderless or vocal lumpen elements in it take over the leadership. On many occasions, we find that established political leaders disappear once the violence starts or once the clashes between the mob and the police start.

A frenzied mob expresses itself through shouting, shaking of fists and uncontrolled body movements. Often, the voice of the person addressing the mob cannot be heard above the din and each member of the mob makes his own interpretation on what the speaker is saying. Each member reconstructs his own version of the lost sounds. Suggestion becomes a more successful method of explaining events than logic. Rumours, as an alternative, substitute definite information. The more active members of the mob use their own suggestions and vocal and physical expressions to convince less active ones to follow their lead.

Proneness to cruelty is another essential feature of a mob. In his private life, an individual member of a mob cannot even think of the violent behaviour that he is willing to adopt as a member of the mob. Even a peaceful or relatively peaceful group of people can commit violent acts when they merge into a mob. In the Indian context, we can find examples falling into this category in the collective violence committed by women, Buddhists and even Jains. As violence in our society is becoming a greater reality day by day, the collective violence of mobs is also increasing. The most horrifying example of increasing cruelty in median contemporary history is the massacre of more than 4000 Sikhs in Delhi and other towns in just two to three days, following the assassination of Smt. Indira Gandhi on 30th October, 1984. These murders were committed entirely by frenzied mobs by the most cruel possible means. Sikhs were burnt alive. While they were burning, the rioters would encircle them, clapping their hands and dancing. Left to themselves most of the members of the crowd would not have been able to witness such a gory scene, let alone participate in it.

The celebrated social thinker, Dr. Ram Manohar Lohia, has described the behaviour of an average Indian member of a crowd as cruel cowardice. We see examples of this behaviour every day. At a bus stop a defenceless pickpocket is beaten to death by the crowd; a woman, declared a witch, is burnt to death by fellow villagers; a local tough beats up a weak person in front of the entire neighbourhood and the only reaction of the spectators is to lock themselves in their homes; a miserable thief is caught and beaten to pulp—these are everyday occurrences in our society. The streak of cruel cowardice hidden in the average Indian, turns into unspeakable brutality when he becomes a part of the mob.

In the congested areas inhabited by Muslims, where large numbers congregate in public places and on the streets throughout day and night, people wandering around aimlessly can effortlessly and naturally become part of a mob that can be easily incited to violence. That is why it is relatively easier to incite violence in a Muslim neighbourhood than it is in a Hindu neighbourhood. The *Hindutva* forces ascribe the permanent presence of crowds in Muslim areas to reasons like the inherent anarchic and violent nature of the community. Actually there are social and economic reasons behind the presence of these people outside their homes, and without understanding these reasons, we cannot understand the behaviour of a Muslim crowd.

Residential areas in Indian society have developed on the basis of religion and castes for historical reasons. Eating habits, customs and rituals, fear of pollution and reasons of security have combined in creating very sharp dividing lines between communally organised residential areas, in urban and rural places of habitation. Even in areas where there are no Muslims, caste determines location of various groups of people and in a locality inhabited only by Muslims, areas are divided according to professions and socio-economic status. This situation has remained largely unchanged after independence.

A large section of the Muslim middle class went to Pakistan after partition, in search of a better future. This group included professionals like lawyers, doctors, teachers, businessmen and industrialists. The absence of these sections left a particular imprint on the development of residential areas. A large middle class influences a community at many levels. This includes the priorities that a community assigns to civic amenities like architecture, drainage, sewerage, and parks. The loss of their middle class status has made the average Muslim neighbourhood the dirtiest and foulest smelling area in any city. Areas crushed by the combined force of poverty, ignorance and uncontrolled population growth, turn into a peculiar world. Insecurity and frequent communal riots in the country have made it impossible for Muslims to move to more open and less congested areas and force them to adjust, by dividing and subdividing the same houses and sharing the existing amenities, generation after generation.

One of the many socio-economic reasons responsible for the presence of a large number of people on the streets in these areas, people who at the slightest provocation can turn into an uncontrolled mob, is the lack of sufficient room for all the members of the family at any particular time in their own houses.

For the purpose of the study, two large Muslim areas were selected to understand the psychology of a Muslim mob. The two areas were Nakhaskohna in Allahabad and Madanpura in Banaras. These areas have some common features prompting their choice. Both areas are very congested Muslim localities and if each is taken as the nucleus of an area of three to four kilometres radius around it, we will find that these contain such social, economic and political factors which can be used to engineer communal rioting. In addition, both areas become the focal points of Muslim reaction at times of communal tension, in the two most sensitive districts of Uttar Pradesh—Allahabad and Banaras.

One of the old residential areas of Allahabad, Nakhaskohna is the centre of Muslim presence. Around it are the congested Muslim localities of Shahgunj, Atala, Chakiya, Mutthigunj, Ranimandi, Mirza Ghalib Road, and Nurulla Road. Lakhs of *beedi*-workers live in these areas. These are the areas having the largest number of T.B. affected persons in the city. Basic amenities like drinking water and toilets are either absent from most homes or practically insufficient. Usually, families are large and each child is looked upon as a source of income. The education of children is, therefore, the most neglected sphere. Sending a child to school means not only depriving the family of what he could earn making *beedies* but also that a portion of the reduced family income will have to be spent on school fees. Naturally, the children are put to the work of making *beedies* at an early age. In most houses, only one room is available for the whole family to sleep in. The reasons for the shortage of space have been discussed earlier. The people living here have little or no opportunity to move to other localities. Some schemes to allow Muslims to live in a cleaner and more open environment like the nearby Karely scheme do exist, but these are completely inadequate for fulfilling the accommodation requirements of the increasing Muslim population. That is why their bulging population has to adjust within the existing accommodation. As a result, each increase in family size or division of a family home results in further reduction of the amenities available. These amenities include the minimum basic needs like a sleeping place for each person, toilets and drinking water. In the course of the survey, a terrifying truth came to the fore. Most middle class and lower class houses just did not have sufficient floor space for all members of the family to lie down and sleep at the same time. It is impossible to conceive of any privacy in these houses even for an intimate act like sex. Most of the inmates sleep in shifts which means that at all times, some people are outside the house while others are inside. This explains the crowds in the streets at all times of the day.

Conditions in Madanpura (Banaras), are more or less the same. It is surrounded by congested Muslim localities on either side of the road going from Godowlia to Lanka. These are both Hindu and Muslim areas, the only difference being that each area is shrunk into itself. The Muslim population here is mostly dependent on sari weaving for employment. Here, too, every child is seen as an additional source of income and the attitude towards educating children is the same as in Nakhaskohna. The result is that in Madanpura there are always crowds of people congregating in small groups on the streets.

From a sociological points of view, the permanent existence of crowds in the streets like Madanpura and Nakhaskohna is very important for the study of communal riots. The crowd facilitates the participation of the community in different kinds of social activities. An interesting fact that came across in the course of this study was that in Allahabad, the participation and achievements of Muslim boys in night cricket and carom board competitions surpassed that of Hindu boys. The reasons for this are obvious. In the Muslim localities, the raised platforms in front of the shops are used for playing carom board all day and night. In addition to the four players, each carom board attracts a small crowd of onlookers. The players and onlookers keep changing, but the game continues. This scene can be witnessed at any time of the day or night in these areas. In Allahabad, carom tournaments are held throughout the year and it is not surprising that most of these are won by Muslim boys. Similarly, at all times of the year, night cricket is played in most Muslim localities, barring times of communal tension.

These easily available crowds are used as fodder by communal organisations for rioting. These crowds comprise illiterate or semi-literate Muslims, who can be easily provoked. Most of them are unemployed or only semi-employed. Those who are employed have professions like beedi-making or weaving which give them no security and make them work for long hours at very low wages. This crowd is, therefore, full of resentment and anger. Lack of cleanliness, sanitation, the acute shortage of elementary civic amenities and complete insecurity are causes which make the crowds in such areas naturally prone to human weaknesses like anarchy, illogical behaviour and anger. In addition to this, the crowd has absolutely no faith in the state. All this leads to a situation which can react aggressively to any provocative incident that occurs.

Indian society can get rid of this situation only when Muslims are able to leave their ghettoes by the development of mixed localities. This process started after 1971, but firstly such mixed localities are so few and far between as to be almost negligible and secondly, ever increasing communal conflicts have reversed this trend in most cities. In many places mixed localities have been abandoned in favour of ghettoes by Muslims in the wake of communal rioting. Later on in this chapter, we will look at the effect of rioting on the demographic changes in Indian society.

We tried to study the relationship between crowds and riots. One more thing that needs to be underlined is that once the mob has become violent, it is impervious to logic and it behaves like a victim of frenzied hysteria. Members of the crowd lose their individuality and become part of a crowd frenzy. All their sensory perceptions gradually force them to lose their distinctive features and merge themselves in the mob, of which, earlier they were merely a part.

In the Indian context, the reaction of a Hindu and a Muslim crowd *vis-a-vis* the police is entirely different. Violent mobs of organised segments like students, labour and traders can also turn unlawful and attack the police. Similarly, police may also use maximum force to quell these groups but we find a perceptible difference in the pattern of behaviour of the crowd as well as the police, if the crowd is of Muslim students, Muslim labour, or Muslim traders. A distinct feeling of initial distrust is visible in the conduct of both the police and such a crowd. We will discuss the reasons for this inbuilt distrust in the next chapter. This feeling influences the reaction of both. While the Muslim crowd visualises every police action as a negative approach to their feelings, we find the police over-reacting in most of the situations when it comes into confrontation with a Muslim group. The behaviour of the Muslim crowd present at Idgah in Moradabad in 1980 and the use of force by the police in reaction, is a good example of this tendency. In this case, while the Muslims had congregated to offer the *namaz* on Id, they held the police responsible for the entry of a pig into the Idgah grounds. The altercation between the Muslims and the police on this issue led to over-reaction on the part of both with the result that more than a hundred people were killed in subsequent police firing. Were it a Hindu congregation, perhaps the reaction on the part of both would have been different.

The Demographic Changes

Communal riots have strengthened the tendency of the Muslims to remain in ghettoes. After independence, because of the lower incidence of riots till 1960-1961 and the gradual emergence of a Muslim middle class which comprised government employees, traders, industrialists and professionals like doctors and lawyers, which to some extent compensated for the loss of a large section of middle class Muslims who migrated to Pakistan, the number of the middle class Muslims who wanted to migrate from the narrow and dirty lanes of old towns to newly developed, planned and cleaner localities increased. Residential townships developed by various government agencies also helped this process. If we analyse the process of urbanisation in the sixties and seventies, we find that the phenomenon of intense urbanisation had one positive feature and that was the growth of mixed areas. Industrialisation also helped this process.

The mixed areas would have positively affected communal relations in this sub-continent, if only they had been permitted to grow. They would have helped members of both communities to shed their prejudices and to understand each other better. Unfortunately, the unchecked growth of communal riots after 1960 has not only stopped this process but has in fact reversed it. Not only fewer mixed localities are coming up, but in those towns which witnessed frequent communal rioting, such localities are gradually becoming uni-religious and Hindus and Muslims are migrating to 'their' localities.

To study this tendency, Shastrinagar, a locality in Meerut, was chosen. Developed during the last two decades on the Meerut-Hapur road, this colony of hundreds of houses is a fine example of planned urban development. Government agencies have developed this colony after acquiring agricultural land around Meerut town. In the township, both houses and developed plots have been sold to people. The agencies did not experience any difficulty in selling these houses or plots because of the township's close proximity to Delhi and the rapid industrialisation of Western Uttar Pradesh. One significant factor in the development of the colony was that more than two hundred Muslims purchased houses or plots in it. These were professional Muslims who had made money and now aspired to get out of the old Muslim localities and settle in a township which had modern amenities like parks, broad roads, schools, sewers and drainage. Among the early settlers were people like Bashir Badr, a renowned Urdu poet. According to him, in the early days all those who intended to purchase property in this locality were ridiculed by their co-religionists. They were told that though they were going to a mixed locality, they would have to come back to their old places. Initially, very few Muslims opted for the new colony. However, after some time the number rapidly swelled. Before 1987, this area remained almost unaffected by the communal tension which recurred periodically in Meerut but the whole process was reversed in 1987. Almost each Muslim house of this locality, including the house of Bashir Badr, was subjected to mob attacks. The result was that, with very few exceptions, all the Muslims inhabitants went back to Muslim ghettoes. Badr migrated to Bhopal.

The experience of the Kareli scheme in Allahabad is similar. After every riot, one hears of Hindus selling their houses in this newly developed mixed colony which is surrounded by densely populated Muslim localities, and migrating to 'their' areas.

Because of its industrial character, Ahmedabad had many such mixed localities where Hindus and Muslims coexisted until the riots of 1969. Bapunagar, Navrangpura, Chamanpura, Gomtipur, Kalupur, Dariapur were some such areas. After the 1969 riots, Hindus and Muslims living there, started identifying safe places for themselves. If there were some stray Hindu houses in a Muslim dominated pocket, they sold them and purchased houses in Hindu areas. Muslims did the same. This process got accelerated after every riot and was completed by the riots of 1985. Examples contrary to this may be available only as exceptions. Bapunagar is an interesting example of this phenomenon where main roads divide new exclusive areas of the Hindus and the Muslims. During communal tension, one can witness the congregation of both communities on respective side of the road, attacking each other with missiles like stones. Labour colonies, built by the government many decades ago, have also been affected and the labourers residing in these quarters have interchanged their dwellings to move to safer localities.

The metropolitan consciousness of Mumbai was badly shaken in the riots of 1992-93 and this process of relocation has also started there. Takshila colony Andheri (East). Nirmal Nagar of Bandra (East), Chacha Nagar, Kherwadi Municipal colony, Charkap (Kandivali) and North East Bhandup are localities from where Muslims have migrated after selling their property. Similarly, Hindus from Radhabai Chawl of Jogeshwari, Kurla Pipeline Road, Rafiq Nagar in Deonar, Dongri in Central Mumbai have sold their houses and shifted to other places. Normally the displaced families have suffered financial losses in selling and purchasing of property but they preferred to bear with it, considering the threat perception.

Many dangerous consequences will surface in the future if the tendency of demographic changes is not arrested effectively. Understanding about each other, which is already low in our society, will be further reduced by ghettoes. The result would be an increase in prejudices and unfounded perceptions. During violence, these localities will become ideal targets of attack.

Commercial Rivalries

Many a time, we find commercial rivalries as the causes behind communal riots. Hundreds of years of co-existence has helped develop a plural Indian society. This society is so interdependent in its economic activities that it is difficult to visualise a situation where give and take among various sections is non-existent. Especially in areas like handicrafts and cloth-making on looms. Hindu or Muslim entrepreneurs and artisans cannot flourish without each other's assistance. The sari industry of Banaras, lock manufacturing in Aligarh or brassware at Moradabad are some such areas of economic activity where both the communities are so interdependent on each other in the realm of raw material, craftsmanship and marketing, that any bitterness in their relationship would affect the whole industry adversely.

During the last few decades, a perceptible qualitative difference is being felt in even those towns where the economic and commercial interests of the two communities were inseparable. Communal forces have identified certain contradictions in their relationships, to create situations in which rioting is encouraged to further the commercial interests of certain individuals. The sari industry of Banaras is a good example of this trend. Traditionally in this industry, weaving was done by Muslims and the trade was in the hands of Hindu businessmen. These businessmen used to provide raw material to weavers and get the finished product for marketing. During the last few decades a few Muslim weavers have emerged as big traders. If we carefully analyse the causes of certain recent riots, we will find that business rivalries between these traders form the real backgroundfor communial clashes. Because of this factor, we find planned and organised attacks on the looms working for rival traders. As part of this game, the godowns of opponents were looted or efforts were made to implicate influential trade rivals in riot cases.

Similar tendencies are visible in Moradabad also. Before the partition of the country, the industry of brass-ware was mostly in the hands of Muslims. After independence many such Muslims migrated to Pakistan and the leadership of the industry slipped into the hands of the clever and hard-working Punjabi migrants. These new leaders of the industry developed it manifold and it became one of the biggest foreign exchange earners in the state. The commercial rivalry of the Hindu and the Muslim businessmen has led to many riots in this town also. As a result, we find systematic attacks on factories and godowns of business rivals.

During this study, data that emerged regarding the extent of involvement of the land mafia in the recent riots of Ahmedabad is amazing. Better known as the builder lobby, this mafia is entirely non-communal in its structure. Their communal operations are mainly to further commercial interest. Till recently, Ahmedabad had many old localities where mixed populations resided. After 1969, periodic convulsions of communal rioting resulted in the migration of the Hindus and the Muslims to 'safer' localities. People intending to migrate are the first target of this mafia. The *modus-operandi* of the mafia is very simple. They first identify places where exclusive townships for the Hindus and the Muslims could be developed and they start developing these areas. During the time of registration of plots and houses, communal tension is created through systematic efforts. The nervous residents of mixed localities start making a bee-line for registration. Again once the plots and houses are ready for sale and if there has been a slump, communal tension is again created and frightened people again fall prey to it.

Interestingly, it is not necessary that a builder develops property only for his own co-religionists. Likewise, Hindu and Muslim builders may extend credit and muscle power to each other to create tension.

The contribution of the land mafia to communal riots is also visible in Mumbai. Because of the sky-rocketing prices of land, the builder lobby has acquired political and social clout apart from wealth. This mafia can go to any extent to get a piece of land vacated for the construction of a residential or commercial complex. Examples abounded in the riots of 1992-93 where *Chawls* or *Jhuggi Jhopris* in slum areas were burnt, some time along with some of their inhabitants, with the obvious purpose of getting the land vacated. Certain huts in Dharavi were attacked which had already been vacated by their inhabitants along with all their belongings. The purpose of this was very clear. The forces behind such attacks wanted the land to construct new buildings.

In a study conducted by Asghar Ali Engineer about the riots in Hyderabad (1990-91), it was found that the role of land mafia, in collaboration with their political mentors, was decisive in engineering and sustaining these riots for long period. Actually, the riots of December 1990, started with fight between two gangs of land grabers, Muslims and Hindus. It is alleged that the Muslim group had the backing of the Majlis-e-Ittihadul Muslimin and the Congress while the Hindu group did not belong to any party. The city of Hyderabad had been receiving large number of migrants from different parts of the country after independence. The Majlis had the support from the Muslims who had migrated from Maharashtra and Karnataka and the Bhartiya Janata Party tried to win the Hindu migrants coming from Warangal and Nalgonda districts. Due to these migrations, it is estimated that between 1956 and 1984 there was a distress sale of property worth Rs. 50 crores in the old city. Asghar Ali

Engineer's study shows that most of the money was pocketed by unscrupulous elements and shared by rowdies, goondas and politicians.

REFERENCES

1. To justify the massacre of Sikhs after the assassination of Smt. Indria Gandhi, the same rumour was spread in every city that the Sikhs had distributed sweets on hearing of Smt. Gandhi's death and that this had provoked the Hindus into attacks on Sikhs. This rumour could not be substantiated anywhere.
2. In 1946, the massacre of 30,000 Muslims (40-50,000 according to non-official estimates) in Bihar was attributed to the reaction against the reported killing of thousands of Hindus by Muslims in Noakhali where actually 139 Hindus were killed (official feagures 200, according to non-official sources).
3. *A History of Freedom Movement,* Vol. IV, published by Pakistan Historical Society, contains an article of Sharif-al-Mujahid entitled "Communal Riots". According to it, the behaviour of the Hindus in pre-partition India was always violent and unpredictable while the Muslims were always peaceful and generous even in the most trying situations.
4. Election results of 1946 show the faith of large sections of Muslims in the Two- Nation theory.
5. *Report of the Commission of Enquiry into Communal Disturbances at Bhiwandi,* Vol. 1, p. 165.
6. *Ibid.,* p. 173.

4

Record of Neutrality of Indian Police in Handling Communal Riots

Analysis and Interpretation of Data

Indian society would appear to be badly divided on the role and the concept of neutrality of the police during a communal strife. Different segments of society view the impartial intervention of police in a riot in different ways. During this study, mainly three segments of society were interviewed on their perception of police neutrality. Surprisingly, all the members of a particular group had almost identical views on this issue, meaning thereby that members of a group, in spite of their socio-economic differences, had more or less a common perception of police neutrality during communal strife.

It is a common knowledge that in India mostly the poorest of the poor suffer during communal riots. The questionnaire for the riot victims was set keeping in mind the fact that their social, economic and educational background may prove a handicap for them in answering difficult questions loaded with academic jargons. Very simple questions, with clear response options, were framed for them.

Content analysis of the data was done. The findings are reported in the following paragraphs.

Research Question 1

How do you find police during communal riots?

Friend ( ) Enemy ( ) Neutral ( )

Response

This question was put before the riot victims of both the majority and minority communities. Responses of two hundred riot victims from both the communities were analysed.

Minority Riot Victims

Category	*Frequency*
Friend	3 (1.5%)
Enemy	194 (97%)
Neutral	3 (1.5%)

Majority Riot Victims

Category	*Frequency*
Friend	143 (71.5%)
Enemy	13 (6.5%)
Neutral	44 (22%)

It is evident from the responses of the minority and majority communities that their perceptions of police neutrality are diametrically opposed to each other. For an average Muslim, the police during a communal riot is more like an enemy than a friend. This perception is based on certain experiences of the community. We will discuss these experiences in this chapter. Similarly, Hindu perception of the police being their friend in a communal riot situation is also the result of police handling of such riots. We will try to identify the reasons behind such a big difference in the perception of the two communities.

Research Question 2

Will you approach police for help during communal riots?

Yes ( ) No ( ) Can't say ( )

Response

Minority Riot Victims

Category	*Frequency*
Yes	32 (16%)
No	147 (2%)
Can't say	21 (10.5%)

Majority Riot Victims

Category	*Frequency*
Yes	186 (93%)
No	4 (2%)
Can't say	10 (5%)

The normal and logical reaction of a citizen during a situation like a riot, when his life and property are in danger, should be to approach the police. The reasons behind this are very simple. The police is the only visible arm of the state which is present on the street during a communal riot. A large number of Muslims (73.5) refusing to approach the police even during the gravest hour of their lives, indicates their distrust of the police. Their behavioural pattern is fraught with serious consequences. Lack of faith in the police may amount to lack of faith in the state itself. We will try to probe the reasons behind this situation in detail.

Research Question 3

Which force will you like to be deployed in your area during communal riots?

Civil police ( ) PAC ( ) CRPF ( ) Army ( )

Response

Minority Riot Victims

Category	*Frequency*
C.P.	18 (9%)
PAC	6 (3%)
CRPF	102 (51%)
ARMY	74 (37%)

Majority Riot Victims

Category	*Frequency*
C.P.	70 (35%)
PAC	103(51.5%)
CRPF	10 (5%)
ARMY	17 (8.5%)

From the responses it is clear that more Hindus (35%) have faith in the civil police than Muslims have (9%). Similarly, a majority of the Hindus (51.5%) opted for PAC unlike the Muslims (3%). Here it may be clarified that PAC stands for state armed police battalions like BMP or SRP. This was made clear to the riot victims of Bihar (Bhagalpur), Gujarat (Ahmedabad) and Maharastra (Mumbai). Muslims had more faith in CRPF (51%) and Army (37%). The term CRPF stands for all central police organisations like BSF, ITBP and this was explained to the respondents. The lack of faith in the police and the armed police forces is due to the typical relationship between the Muslims and these forces which will be discussed.

Research Question 4

What will you expect from police during riots?

(*a*) Firm and ruthless handling of rioters ( )

(*b*) Firm and impartial dealing without any discrimination ( )

(*c*) Soft Pedalling ( )

Response

Minority Riot Victims

Category	*Frequency*
a	28 (14%)
b	172 (86%)
c	—

Majority Riot Victims

Category	*Frequency*
a	127 (63.5%)
b	59 (29.5%)
c	14 (7%)

This question was very important in the sense that two almost identical options were given as (a) and (b). Hindu and Muslim riot victims reacted differently to these options. A majority of the Hindus (63.5%) wanted the police to be ruthless and firm with the rioters while Muslims (86) preferred a firm and impartial dealing. We have earlier discussed the belief firmly entrenched in the psyche of the

Hindus that the Muslims, being violent by nature, initiate the riots. Hence, their support to firm and ruthless handling of rioters means to them firm and ruthless handling of the Muslims. On the other hand, Muslims do not have faith in the neutrality of the police, hence, they opted more for impartial handling of rioters.

From a sociological point of view, it may not have been proper to keep police officials in one group, because in spite of wearing the same *Khaki,* their conduct and thinking is distinctly influenced by their social, economic and geographical background. But, they have been kept in one group for the purposes of this study, because the process of their training and the expectation of the society from them to behave in an organised and disciplined manner affects their thought process in such a way that they start reacting on social issues, to a large extent, in a similar manner. For example, naxalism or terrorism, for most of the police officials, is only a law and order problem. They believe with full sincerity that if law and order is enforced strictly, the nation can get rid of these problems. Similarly, communalism is also more or less a law and order problem for them.

During this study, fifty serving and retired police officials were interviewed. Some of them were interviewed face to face, while the questionnaire was sent to the others. The officers who were interviewed included some of the stalwarts of the Indian Police.—N.S. Saxena, K.F. Rustomjee, J.F. Rebeiro, J.N. Chaturvedi and B.K. Roy who have reacted on the issues related to the perception of police neutrality. Most of them have had wide exposure to this problem and many of them have been contributing regularly to various journals and newspapers on this issue.

The following questions put to them, covered various aspects of police neutrality. The questions and analysis of their responses are given below.

Unlike the questions put to the riot victims, these questions were descriptive in nature.

Research Question-1

How will you define the concept of police neutrality?

Response

Almost all the respondents were convinced that police neutrality during a communal strife means impartial and unbiased handling of a communal situation. Some of the salient features emphasised by the respondents were :

(*i*) Action without getting affected by the communal feelings;

(*ii*) Function in a manner that is perceived to be neutral by general public; and

(*iii*) Impartial action strictly according to law.

Research Question-2

Have you ever noticed a communal bias in the behaviour of policemen during a communal riot? You may like to elaborate this point with some personal experience.

Response

The question was specific hence, it is possible to categorise responses in yes or no.

Category	*Frequency*
Yes	22 (48%)
No	23 (52%)

We find police officers evenly divided on this issue. It was observed that officers from the South were almost unanimous in their belief that the virus of communalism has not affected policemen. Officers from the North, or those states where communal riots have become a regular phenomenon, admitted the policemen behaving in a communal manner.

Research Question-3

Do you think that construction of mandir, mosque, gurudwara or a church in a police line or police station is correct?

Response

Category	*Frequency*
Yes	29 (58%)
No	21 (42%)

It is clear that the majority of police officers did not find any objections to having places of worship in a police establishment. The main reason behind this response was that most of the policemen are deeply religious and the absence of a place of worship in the lines would force them to go outside, which would result in avoidable expenditure of time and dislocation of their duty hours.

Research Question-4

Do you think that use of religious symbols by exhibiting portraits/photographs of deities and gods in police offices or using of *shlokas* of Gita on police sign boards as is the case with U.P. Police or performing *pujas* or breaking of coconuts during police functions, should be discouraged in day-to-day functioning of police?

Response

While 26 officers supported discontinuation of such practices, 24 found no harm in these religious symbols being associated with police functioning. It is clear that a smaller percentage of officers (48%) supported display of religious symbols in day-to-day police working than those who were in favour of having a place of worship in police lines/stations (58%). Perhaps they differentiated between a place of worship in one corner of the lines and open display of religious symbols in offices/police stations, which are visited by a large number of outsiders.

Communal Expectations of the Society

Before we analyse the reasons behind the perception of the minorities of the police as an enemy during communal riots, we should keep the unfortunate fact in our mind that the general expectations of Indian society of the police, which was born as an organised and modern institution during the British regime, has mostly been communal. An average Hindu or Muslim policeman is perceived as the protector of the interest of his community. These expectations increased with the increase of communalism in Indian society. A Hindu or Muslim complainant visiting a police station could establish a better rapport with his co-religionist policemen and the actions of policemen belonging to another religion would appear to him untrustworthy and hostile.

These communal expectations from the police are mainly the result of the large scale communalisation of Indian society by the British state as a means of protecting its interests. All the segments of society were affected by this process and it was but natural that the police, which hailed from the same society, also could not remain untouched. On many occasions, we find the conduct of the police that of trying to come up to the communal expectations of the society. Before we analyse the hostile relationship between the minorities and the police in contemporary society, it would be useful to discuss two incidents which occurred in pre-Independence India which will help us understand as to how much our society expected from an average policeman to stand for the communal interests of his community.

Incidents of communal rioting took place in the rural areas of the Eastern part of Bengal in the first two decades of this century. Gradually this violence acquired political overtones in the third and fourth decades. Initially this conflict was basically the outcome of the efforts of Muslim communalists to use the economic exploitation of the Muslim peasantry by Hindu landlords and money lenders, for communal movements. The anger of the Muslim peasantry against the exploitative behaviour of these landlords and moneylenders could take a communal turn because of the religious symbols used by the *maulvis* to incite them.

It will be very interesting to study the role of policemen in this process of communalising the socio-economic conflicts of the illiterate and gullible villagers of East Bengal. The communal forces had very systematically spread two rumours to mobilise the Muslim peasantry against the Hindus. The first rumour was that an agreement had been reached between the British monarch and the Nawab of Dhaka according to which an attack on the Hindus would be considered an act of loyalty to the British Empire. According to the second rumour, no prosecution would be launched for attacks on the Hindus during a particular period. This period was different in various regions.

To give credibility to this rumour, *mullas* took the help of the police. It is not surprising that, with the status which a policeman enjoyed in contemporary society, it was easier to make an innocent villager believe the rumours if these were confirmed by a police official. Since the Muslims were in a majority in the Bengal police, the task of Muslim communalists became easy. During violence at various places, complaints not only of Muslim policemen being in collusion with the Muslim rioters were made in large numbers but the most serious charges were made regarding their involvement in spreading and making the villagers believe these rumours.

During a trial, when a Muslim villager was charged for rioting against the Hindus, he raised his finger towards a Muslim constable present in the court and with all the innocence at his command, told the court that it was this man who had given him to understand that according to a pact between the British Queen and the Nawab of Dhaka, this action was to be considered as loyalty to the Raj and no punishment was to be meted out if it was committed within a stipulated period.

The letter of C.Y. Chintamani, editor of *Leader*, published from Allahabad, addressed to the Chief Secretary, United Provinces, also throws light on the communal expectations of society from the police. Chintamani, who was also a member of the Legislative Council, enclosed a long petition of one Pt. Raghubar Dayal Vaidya of Kanpur along with his letter. In his petition, Pt. Raghubar Dayal had in detail lamented how Kanpur, which was an important centre of Hindu businessmen, had become totally insecure for Hindus. The only reason, according to him, for this growing insecurity was the overwhelming representation of the Muslims in the Kanpur police. The majority of Muslims as SHOs of police stations and at various important assignments was detrimental to the Hindu interests. It is revealed from the comments of the IGP sent to the Chief Secretary on this petition, that the representation of Muslims in the civil police, all over the United Provinces (and not only in Kanpur) was more than that of the Hindus. The reason behind this was Urdu as the medium of the departmental promotion examinations. The petition of Raghubar Dayal and the comments of IGP are available in Appendix 'D'.

In fact, the apprehensions expressed by Pt. Reghubar Dayal against the over-representation of the Muslims in the police force at Kanpur, were nothing but another form of communal expectations of Indian society from the police. According to these expectations, a *Khaki*-clad police functionary was ultimately viewed either as a friend of his community or the enemy of the other community.[1]

During the last few decades, Indian society has been affected by the communal virus on a very large scale. It is very natural that the police has also got infected. During the first few years after independence, when politics was guided by values like selfless service and the building of a great nation, the spirit of patriotism and enthusiasm were visible in all walks of Indian life. Later on, when politics started decaying, the impact of this was felt by other institutions and the Indian people, at large, became frustrated. One can feel the perceptible impact of this on the graph of communal riots. Barring the riots immediately after partition, rioting almost stopped after the assassination of Mahatma Gandhi in the beginning of 1948. The nation, on a march forward through the period of the first five year plan, did not provide much opportunity to the rabid communal forces to raise their heads. These forces remained latent but unfortunately could not be crushed completely. As politics and other institutions got corrupted, the patriotic favour in the masses also got weakened. As a result, communal forces strengthened their base. We find a new wave of communal riots in the beginning of the sixties. The major riots of Jabalpur and about a dozen other towns in the year 1961 were indications of increasing communal feelings and of the dangers facing Indian society.

The more this communalisation increased, the more we find communal riots becoming an integral part of Indian society. Society, badly affected by the communal virus, has once again started expressing its communal expectations from the police. Unfortunately an average policeman is seen trying hard to come up to this expectation. There is definitely a basic flaw in the recruitment and training policies in as much as a policeman continues to be a Hindu or Muslim, in spite of his wearing *Khaki.* How this *Khaki* is affected by the Hindu or the Muslim inhabiting it, can be seen in most of the riots after independence. Only two examples will be sufficient here.

The massacre of the Sikhs after the assassination of Mrs. Indira Gandhi would not have been possible if the police in various towns had not displayed deliberate negligence. At many places, civil liberty organisations accused the police of siding with the rioters. During the course of this study, I came across a very tragic example of the police turning Hindu during these riots. In Kanpur, the Punjabi writer and principal of a college, Ms. Taran Gujral, while narrating her harrowing experience of those days, stated to me that while her locality was surrounded by a frenzied mob and an armed attack was imminent, when she telephoned the police control room for help, all she could get was a derisive laughter and a curt reply from the other side "*Hum bhi to Hindu hain* (after all, we are also Hindus)". This reply to a hapless woman reveals the fact that even after wearing *Khaki,* a policeman can retain his Hindu identity, which is certainly not a liberal but a communal one. The Jagmohan Reddy commission, inquiring into the riots of 1969 in Ahmedabad, has cited more than half a dozen instances where Muslim religious places adjoining the policelines or police stations were attacked and damaged. The argument of the police officers that due to their being busy in quelling riots at various places, these police locations were deprived of sufficient strength and hence, the attack on these religious places could not be prevented, did not impress the commission. Not a single attack on any Hindu place of worship near a police station was reported. One instance of men from the Raikhad policelines attacking a nearby Muslim locality Syed Bara was also brought to the notice of the commission. The commission did not accept the plea of the police officials that the Muslims first attacked the policelines and that the injuries received by them occurred in the course of this attack.[2] One specific example is available in the riots of Bhagalpur (1989) where policemen came out of the policelines and attacked and looted an adjoining Muslim locality. These two situations are examples of the police remaining Hindu in a situation when they are expected to behave impartially.

Bias in Police Actions

We have seen earlier during this study that the perception by Muslims of the police in a communal riot is that of an enemy. If we combine this perception and the communal expectations of pre-independence society from the police, we can understand the truth better. We have found that Muslim policemen were party to spreading of false rumours by fanatics of their community. We have also come across the apprehensions of the Hindus of Kanpur, expressed in the petition of Pt. Raghubar Dayal, that if a communal violence breaks out in the town, the Muslim police will not protect them. These two happenings represent the dominant trend present in Indian society of that time. We will have to examine the fears in the minds of the minorities keeping these facts in mind. Could it be that the behaviour of the police and the reaction of the minorities at present is just an extension of the earlier trend? Is the perception of the Muslims regarding the police based on certain realities or is the behaviour of the Muslims to be blamed for it? How is it that the perceptions of the Hindus and Muslims are diametrically opposed to each other? We can find the answers of these questions in the behaviour of the police combating communal riots, the representation of the minorities in the police and the conflicting expectations of different segments of society in any given situation.

We should first analyse the efforts of the police to quell an incident of communal violence. Like any other problem of law and order, the efforts of the police to deal with this situation can also be divided into many stages. Collection of intelligence, preventive actions like detention of anti-social and communal elements execution of bonds, instilling fear in the minds of mischief mongers through show of force or diffusing tension through reconciliatory measures may be included in the first stage of the police strategy. The second stage of police action begins with the eruption of violence. This will include actual use of force like lathi-charge or firing, arrests, imposing curfew and extension of protection to the victims of violence. The third and the final stage of the involvement of the police will be in the shape of measures like investigation and prosecution of riot cases, rehabilitation of riot victims, necessary arrangements to ensure that there is no recurrence of communal violence, while building of confidence in the minds of the people.

The neutrality of police behaviour and its relationship with the members of different communities can be defined better only after analysing police actions under the above-mentioned three categories. It is basically the behaviour of the police in communal strife which makes the members of a minority community like the Muslims view it as an enemy. In the subsequent portions of this study we will try to analyse the reasons which are responsible for the police being perceived as an enemy or a friend by two different groups in one identical situation.

We have observed in the last chapter that in most of the major communal riots in the country, Muslims are the worst sufferers both in terms of loss of life and property. In a majority of the riots, the percentage of Muslim casualties is more than 60% of the total. The losses of this community in terms of property would be of a similar proportion. If we keep these hard facts in mind, it will be quite natural to expect that the law enforcing agencies have reacted in a manner which is commensurate with this reality. Unfortunately, the real picture is completely different. In most of the riots where the number of Muslims killed was many times more than the Hindus, it was they who were mainly arrested, searches were conducted mostly in their houses and curfew was also imposed in a harsher manner in their localities. This observation holds even in those riots where those killed were almost all Muslims *e.g.* Ahmedabad (1969), Bhiwandi (1970) and Bhagalpur (1989). This phenomenon can be better understood through the table given below:

		Arrests and Casualties	***Hindu***	***Muslim***
Bhiwandi (1970)	Riots	Arrested in Cognisable/ Substantive offences	21	901
		Casualities	17	59
Merrut (1982) up to 15th September1982	Riots	Arrested in cognisable/ substantive offences	124	231
		Casualties	2	8

Similarly, in house searches, we find the Muslims at the receiving end. This is the general pattern during a communal riot: a Muslim *mohalla* is cordoned off with the help of the army or para military forces and then all the houses are searched indiscriminately. The entire community finds its pride injured by such acts. A very interesting mind-frame is displayed by the civil and police administration. While the curfew is enforced with all strictness in Muslim localities, it is virtually confined to the main roads in Hindu areas, the normal activities of life remain unaffected in the lanes and by-lanes in these areas. While I was interviewing the riot victims of Ahmedabad, Meerut, Mumbai and Allahabad, this single factor transpired to be one of the most decisive as far as the anger of the Muslims towards the police is concerned. This complaint of discrimination was more bitter in areas where there were adjoining Hindu and Muslim residential townships. The meaning of curfew was different for the poor residents of slum areas belonging to the two communities in Ahmedabad and Allahabad. During my visit I found that most houses lacked facilities like drinking water and lavatories. The Muslims had a general complaint that while they were not permitted to move out of their houses to fetch water from the public taps, which happen to be the main source of water supply in such areas, the Hindus were not subjected to such restrictions.

It would be revealing to analyse the number of victims of police firing in communal riots. Normally it is the Muslims who suffer the brunt of police firing. The perusal of the table given below will be interesting in the sense that we will find the Muslims suffering more in police firing even in those riots where they have already suffered much more than the Hindus in the violence.

Name of Riot	*No. of persons killed in police firing*	
	Hindu	*Muslim*
Bhiwandi (1970)	Nil	9
Firozabad (1972)	Nil	6
Aligarh (Sep.-Oct. 1978)	Nil	7
Meerut (1982)	Nil	6

It is not very difficult to identify reasons behind the discriminatory behaviour of the police. The conduct of an average policeman is guided by those predetermined beliefs and misconceptions which influence the mind of an average Hindu. We have already discussed in detail the beliefs which an average Hindu carries in his mind regarding conflicts between the two major communities of the country. Like an average Hindu, an average Hindu policeman also believes that Muslims, generally, are cruel and violent by nature. In the course of my study, I spoke to a large number of policemen working in various ranks. I was amazed to find that most of them seriously believed, that apart from being cruel and violent, Muslims were untrustworthy, anti-national and easily influenced by fanatical leadership and could indulge in rioting at the slightest provocation.

During my study, I found that generally the policemen were in agreement that Muslims initiated riots. When I confronted many of them with the question that since Muslims suffered more, then why should they start a riot, they replied with arguments that an average Hindu would preffer.

It is but natural that after being convinced of the mischievous role of the Muslims in riots, most policemen do not have any doubts regarding the ways and means to check them. They sincerely believe that there is only one way to control a riot and that is to crush the mischief mongering Muslims. Whenever an instruction is received from the state government or senior police officials to deal with the rioters firmly and ruthlessly, these instructions are interpreted in a prejudiced and biased way. Firmness and ruthlessness towards rioters is interpreted as firmness and ruthlessness towards the Muslims. The various forms of firmness have distinct meanings; arrest means arrests of Muslims; search means searches of Muslim houses and police firing means firing on the Muslims.

How strongly our sub-conscious is affected by our prejudices and predetermined beliefs and how much our conduct is influenced by these, is obvious from the actions of the policemen during communal riots. Even in those riots, where Muslims started suffering from the very inception of rioting or where the killings of the Muslims was totally one sided, the policemen who were posted there, gave a very interesting picture of their way of thinking. It is not only during riots that they would believe that the riot was caused by mischieves of the Muslims, even much later, when it has been established that the Muslims suffered most, they present many arguments to prove that the Muslims were responsible for the riots. While talking to some of the policemen who were posted in Bhagalpur (1989) and Mumbai (1992-93), I was amazed to find that the perception of the Muslims being violent and cruel was so deeply inbuilt in their psyche that even after admitting the disproportionate destruction of Muslim life and property, they had many 'reasons' to deny the suggestion that 'naturally non-violent and pious Hindus' were in any way responsible for the damage to the Muslims.

It is this psychology of the policemen which guides their reactions during communal strife. While combating riots, they start searching for friends among the Hindus and foes among the Muslims. It is a common sight in the towns of Northern India that the reinforcements sent from outside, during communal tensions, make their lodging arrangements in temples, *dharmshalas* and parks in Hindu localities or the space available in Hindu homes and shops. When the shops are closed during curfew, food, tea and snacks are supplied to them by Hindu homes. Members of the majority community, who in normal times may keep a distance from the police just like the members of the minority communities do, they suddenly see policemen as friends during communal tensions. It is their natural expectations of a 'friendly' police that it will not use force against them. Whenever, the police uses force against the Hindus, their reaction is that of an amazed and cheated group.

The FIR lodged by Ajit Dutta, DIG during the riots of Bhagalpur (1989), very candidly underlines this mentality. This FIR is available in Appendix 'E'. Its perusal reveals the interesting incident of a law-breaking mob of the Hindus, congregating on the road during curfew hours, expressing its dismay and anger when. Dutta threatened them with police firing. I am reminded of a similar personal experience at Allahabad (1980) when in Gadiwan Tola, I warned a Hindu mob bent upon rioting, that we would open fire if they did not disperse, I found that the crowd did not take it seriously at first and thought it was a joke, subsequently when they heard me ordering a Head constable to open fire from his carbine, there was a clear look of disbelief and surprise in their eyes.

How far this deeply entrenched perception of the Muslims being solely responsible for the riots and strict behaviour towards them being the only way to quell a riot, affects the reactions of a policeman, may be illustrated with the example of Hashimpura where the savagery and horrifying non-professionalism of the police behaviour was a matter of national shame.

The riots in Meerut (1987) were unprecedented in the toll of human life and for the long period of continued and unabated violence. The magnitude of the riot which started on May 17, 1987, can be gauged from the fact that to deal with it, the services of about 50 gazetted Police Officers and Magistrates along with more than 70 companies of PAC, para military forces and army were pressed in. The policemen deployed there harboured all the above mentioned beliefs and prejudices. When their tremendous round-the-clock vigil could not control the violence, some of them resorted to an action which could have not been imagined. Being fully convinced that the riots in a civilised society could be ended only by teaching the Muslims a lesson, one section of the

PAC picked up more than two dozen Muslims from a locality known as Hashimpura on the 22nd of May, where house to house searches were going on, and killed them at two places in Ghaziabad, after transporting them there in one of police trucks.

I was S.P. Ghaziabad at that time. After receiving the information, I got two cases registered against the PAC. The cases were handed over to the Uttar Pradesh CID and, after eight years of investigations, a charge sheet I was filed against the erring personnel of the PAC, in 1995.

Why should the PAC commit such a detestable act? I had the opportunity to talk to a large number of policemen deployed in Meerut in this period during my tenure as S.P. Ghaziabad (1985-88) as well as during the course of the present study. I wanted to understand the motivating factors behind such a heinous offence.

The analysis of the psychology of these men will help us appreciate the relationship between the police and members of the minority communities. Most of the policemen posted in Meerut in 1987 thought that the riots were the result of Muslim mischief. They were also of the opinion that Meerut had become a mini-Pakistan because of the stubbornness of the Muslims, and that it was necessary to teach them a lesson in order to establish permanent peace in Meerut. They were badly affected by rumours which suggested that the Hindus in Meerut were totally vulnerable to Muslim attacks. Their belief that Muslims of Meerut deserved. a suitable lesson resulted in Hashimpura.

Instances like Hashimpura worsen the inimical relationship between Muslims and the police. This relationship is clearly visible during communal tensions. We find that many riots start with a Muslim attack on the police. Quite often the presence of the police in a surcharged atmosphere fills muslims with anger. Reacting to the demolition of the Babri Mosque in Ayodhya, angry mobs of the Muslims in other cities venting their feelings of resentment on the street, initially chose the police as their targets rather than the Hindus. There are many examples of communal rioting in which the trouble started as a clash between the police and the Muslims and then turned into a Hindu-Muslim conflict. The Idgah incident of Moradabad (1980) is an important example of this trend.

The most interesting example of the hostile relationship between the Muslims and the police can be found in the behaviour of a police party entering a Muslim locality during communal tensions. The briefing, preparation and weaponry of this party intending to enter a Muslim locality for arrests or searches or even normal patrolling is such that it appears that it is going to enter in an enemy territory. I have seen many such groups and always found them comprising people full of apprehensions and fears. Their behaviour is not without reason. Alertness on their part is necessary as they may be attacked at any time. Who is responsible for this feeling of distrust and enmity? Perhaps the seeds are to be found in the terms 'We and They' used by police officials for the Hindus and the Muslims during their conferences organised to devise ways and means to deal with a communal situation.

Reporting of facts, investigation into and prosecution of participants in communal riots is another area where we find clear communal bias in police behaviour. The reporting of facts is done at various levels. Intelligence reports being prepared at the level of police stations and intelligence inputs to be sent to government and senior police formations are normally affected by this bias. For example, I have found one interesting thing in the lists of communal agitators being maintained at various police levels in Uttar Pradesh. For most of the officials, responsible for maintaining such lists, a communal agitator means a Muslim communal agitator. Even during those days when Hindu communal forces were active in the movement of Ram Janambhoomi, it was very difficult to find the names of Hindu inciters in the list. Perhaps the same perception that holds that to be communal is the prerogative of the Muslims, was at work here.

What damage this bias can inflict on police professionalism can be understood from the incident of the destruction of the Babri mosque. It is evident from the charge a sheet filed by the CBI that the demolition of the mosque was the result of well planned conspiracy. None of the intelligence agencies could report this fact before the 6th of December, 1992.

A very heinous example of this bias in reporting facts is available at Bhagalpur (1989) riots where, 116 Muslims were killed in village Logain on the 27th of October, 1989. This brutal massacre was enacted by the Hindus of Logain and the neighbouring villages. Logain village is 26 kilometres from the district headquarters of Bhagalpur with police station only four kilometres away at Jagdishpur. The Muslims killed were buried in the fields and cauliflower plants were grown in them. Out of 181 Muslim inhabitants of the village, 65 survivors and their attackers went to many places including Bhagalpur town and reported this ghastly incident. Details were published in local and national newspapers. In spite of this, the district and police administration of Bhagalpur kept denying any such happening till the 8th of December, 1989, when a police party led by DIG Ajit Dutta, dug out some of the dead bodies from the fields.

The Justice D.P. Madon Commission, which enquired into the riots of 1970 at Bhiwandi-Jalgaon, cited many examples of bias in reporting. It is very clear in its opinion regarding the failure of the police to take effective measures at Jalgaon even after receiving the reports of Bhiwandi troubles: "The real reason for the inadequacy of the measures taken by the authorities was the communal bent of mind of some officers and incompetence of others... Unfortunately, S.P., S.T. Raman appears to have possessed a communal bent of mind and perhaps a pro-Janasangh bias. As shown by some of his own reports and his noting on reports of Inspector Sawant, Incharge of the Jalgaon city police station, he fully realised the seriousness of the situation. He, however, chose to turn a blind eye to it and even to mislead the government and the IGP about the true state of affairs in his report dated 29th March, 1970".[3]

The Commission finds a similar bias in the conduct of PSI Bhalerao, which resulted in his non-reporting of incidents of brick-batting by the Hindus, in the records of the police station.[4] The officials of the intelligence department displayed similar bias. PSI Badgoojar had sent an entirely false report to DIG (INT) that the riot was caused by the Muslims throwing burning torches on Hindu houses.

We find investigating agencies full of communal bias while investigating riot cases. We have the classic case of Hashimpura, Meerut (1989), cited above in which U.P. CID took eight years to complete the investigation of a case which is unparalleled in its savagery and lack of professionalism. We can quote another example of bias in investigations in the cases registered during the 1984 anti-Sikh riots. In most of these cases, police organisations of various states have failed to book the culprits.

LBS National Academy of Administration, Mussoorie, has conducted a very interesting study in this context. According to a reading material supplied by the Academy to the trainee probationers, during disturbances in Meerut

(1982), 71 FIRs were recorded during the period 7th to 15th of September, 1982, and 55 FIRs were recorded during the period 24th to 30th of September. Details of FIRs between the period 15th September and 24th September or after 1st October, 1982, were not available. An analysis was done of the 189 FIRs about which details are available. Out of these, 18 FIRs are related to offences u/s 302 IPC and/or 307 IPC. These could be termed as the most heinous offences. The rest are related to minor offences or preventive actions. Efforts were made to divide the 18 FIRs relating to murder/attempt to murder into two categories, one in which the Muslims were alleged to be aggressive and the other in which the Hindus were allegedly aggressive. The pattern of arrest in such cases was as follows:

Where Muslims were allegedly aggressive				Where Hindus were allegedly aggressive			
Arrested		Killed		Arrested		Killed	
Hindus	Muslims	Hindus	Muslims	Hindus	Muslims	Hindus	Muslims
23	232	2		7			

The special investigation squad, set up to investigate the riot cases of Bhiwandi, was cited by the Madon Commission as a glaring example of communal bias. The efforts by the investigation squad to establish a theory of conspiracy by the Muslims was ridiculed by the commission, which found it totally untenable. The commission has cited many examples of investigators trying to fabricate evidence against Muslims and shielding the Hindus culprits. It also found many examples of tampering with official records in a communally biased manner.[5]

One more important area of communal bias on the part of the state agencies was found in their treatment of arrested persons. It is a well established norm in a civilised society that after a person is taken into custody, it becomes the duty of the state to protect his life and to provide him all such facilities which he is entitled to, as part of his human rights. Unfortunately there are numerous instances when the basic human rights of persons under custody were violated by police and jail officials solely because of their communal bias. Only a few examples will suffice to elaborate this point.

The example of Hashimpura had been discussed in detail. Here persons taken into custody were killed in a cold blooded manner. In the same riot of Meerut (1987) when arrested Muslims were transported by bus from Meerut to Fatehgarh, they were attacked by inmates and jail officials of Fatehgarh Central Jail and six of them died. Nobody, will believe that jail inmates attacked these hapless detenues without the active incitement by the jail officials.

To further elaborate this point, it will be better to quote from the Madon Commission report regarding communal bias in the treatment of prisoners.[6] The evidence placed before the Commission has established the following facts with respect to the treatment meted out to the prisoners:

(1) Some Muslim prisoners were beaten, both when arrested and while in police custody.

(2) There was almost no food or water for the prisoners on May 7 and 8, 1970.

(3) Prisoners were made to sit on the road outside the Bhiwandi police station in the sun, without any shade, as alleged by the Muslim parties.

(4) Muslim prisoners were made to stay in the compound of the *taluka* police station with the shade of trees for only a few of them while Hindu prisoners were made to stay on the verandas.

(5) Discrimination was practised in the distribution of food and water between the Hindu and the Muslim prisoners.

Their (officials) reasons for not sending for the fire-engines to bring drinking water for the prisoners was that most of the prisoners were Muslims and not Hindus and the Hindu prisoners were allowed free access to the water taps at *taluka* police station.

Justice Joseph Vithayathal in his report of the Commission of Inquiry of Tellicherry Disturbances (1971) has underlined the communal bias in the behaviour of policemen in dealing with riots. It will be better to quote some of his observations which need further explanation:

236. *There might also be another reason why the Dy. Superintendent of Police was cautious. He knew what the attitude of the rank and file of the Hindu policemen was towards the Muslims. He says in his evidence that while doing patrol duty he had to curb some of them who could not restrain themselves when they met Muslims on the road. The Sub-Collector also speaks to that effect. (P15W1 at p. 13) Some witnesses say that while chasing away the Muslims found on the way some of these policemen cried out to them to go to Pakistan. At Mattambram one or two of them got into the mosque and besides beating PW6, Usmankuṭty Haji, a very respectable person, broke the tube-lights and chandeliers in the mosque. There is nothing to show that there was any justification for this action.*

245. Some of the victims in the incidents that took place during the third phase of the disturbances and those who witnessed those incidents swear to the fact that policemen were standing nearby when the rioting took place and that they did not do anything either to stop the rioting or to apprehend the culprits. P28 Wl K.P. Kader says that when his house was attacked and while the looting was going on 4-5 policemen were standing on the road at a distance of 10-15 yards. P27 W 2 K.P. Raghavan says that when Muslim houses were attacked at Ponniyam at about noon he went to the Panur Police Station and reported the matter but that the police came only at 5 p.m. and that by that time all the Muslim houses on the road side had been looted. P1 W1 Sri Ramadas says that when he saw Ayisha Manzil at Thiruvangad being attacked he phoned to the police but no police party came to the place. After P.P. Manzil was burnt a party of policemen came in a jeep and the witness asked them to stop the jeep and to have a look at the gutted house. They refused to stop the jeep.

The observations of Madon Commission and Joseph Vithayathal Commission of Inquiry are unfortunately true in most riot situations. One could only wish that these were simply aberrations or exceptions and not the general behaviour of the law enforcing agencies.

REFERENCES

1. File-379 Box-84, Police Department 1936—Source U.P. State Archives.
2. *Report of the Reddy Enquiry Commission*, pp. 173-74.
3. *Report of the Commission of Enquiry into Communal Disturbances at Bhiwandi, Jalgaon and Mahed in May, 1970*, p. 160.
4. *Ibid*, p. 107.
5. *Ibid*, p. 108.
6. *Ibid*, p. 83.

5

Main Findings

The main findings of the present study are as follows:

(a) Police behave partially during most riots. In all the riots discussed in this study, they did not act as a neutral law enforcement agency but more as a 'Hindu' force.

(b) Perceptible discrimination was visible in the use of force, preventive arrests, enforcement of curfew, treatment of detained persons at police stations, reporting of facts and investigation, detection and prosecution of cases registered during riots. The Muslims suffered in all the above mentioned areas.

(c) The perception by the Hindus and the Muslims of the police during communal strife is diametrically opposed. The Hindus view policemen as their friends and protectors during communal riots. The Muslims, by and large, consider policemen their enemies in similar situations.

(d) An average policeman does not shed his prejudices and predetermined beliefs at the time of his entry into the force, and this is reflected in his bias against Muslims during communal violence.

(e) The expectations of the Indian society from an average policeman is communal. The policeman is believed to be a protector of the interests of his community.

(f) The inimical relationship between the police and the Muslims make them over-react in a confrontation like situation.

Recommendations

Communalism is a malaise which infects all sections of society, much more so when there is no tough and effective resistance from the state. Even those parts of the bureaucracy which are supposed to combat communalism are as much infected by preconceived notions and prejudices as any other section of society. There is nothing unnatural about this. The different parts of the machinery of law enforcement hail from various sections of society. It should, therefore, not be surprising that even after joining government services they retain their parochial perceptions about communal riots or social tensions, which they have acquired and continue to acquire as members of society. This reality is no doubt more problematic in the case of the security forces, particularly the police.

To check the problem of communalisation of the police forces and to make them function in a manner that is perceived to be neutral by the general public, and more so by the minority communities, it is necessary that certain basic remedial measures be taken. First of all, the senior leadership of the Indian police should agree, that handling of communal riots is an area which requires a lot of introspection. They may absolve themselves from the allegations of partisan handling of these disturbances but the fact remains that the Indian police, as such does not enjoy the confidence of the minorities and as we have found in this study. In almost every incident of communal strife, it has been accused of displaying a pro-Hindu bias, not only by the Muslim leadership but also by the secular media, social activists and champions of human rights. This failing on the part of the Indian police makes it imperative that remedial measures should not only be drastic but should be taken without delay.

This study suggests four major areas where basic changes are required. These are the recruitment policies for various levels in the police, training interventions, accountability of the police leadership and the involvement of the people in combating communalism. We discuss the four separately.

I. Representation of Minorities in the Police

It is an unfortunate fact that after Independence, the representation of the minorities in the forces has consistently declined. The chart given below clearly indicates that even in communally sensitive provinces, the representation of the minorities has been less than five per cent even while the percentage of the minorities in the overall population of these states is generally between 10 and 15 per cent and, in some case, even higher.[1]

Sl.	*States/UTs*	*Total Police Strength*	*No. of Muslims in Police*	*Percentage of Muslims in Police*
(1)	(2)	(3)	(4)	(5)
1.	Andhra Pradesh	63,147	10,499	16.6
2.	Arunachal Pradesh	4,081	N.A.	N.A.
3.	Assam	43,990	3,936	8.9
4.	Bihar	83,323		
5.	Goa	2,535	73	2.9
6.	Gujarat	63,092	3,897	6.2

(*contd.*)

7.	Haryana	30,431	325	1.7
8.	Himachal Pradesh	1,746	163	1.4
9.	Jammu & Kashmir	40,180	18,045	44.9
10.	Karnataka	49,322	3,557	7.2
11.	Kerala	34,375	3,270	9.5
12.	Madhya Pradesh	88,673	3,720	4.2
13.	Maharashtra	1.58.543	6,633	4.2
14.	Manipur	11,032	934	8.5
15.	Meghalaya	8,271	158	1.9
16.	Mizoram	5,152	699	13.6
17.	Nagaland	14,754	145	0.9
18.	Orissa	36,995	1,029	2.8
19.	Punjab	63,310	210	0.3
20.	Rajasthan	57,167	3,221	5.6
21.	Sikkim	2,732	7	0.2
22.	Tamil Nadu	69,021	3,024	4.4
23.	Tripura	11,161	253	2.3
24.	Uttar Pradesh	1,63875	8,072	4.9
25.	West Bengal	59,137	3,442	5.8
26.	A&N Islands	1,852	111	5.9
27.	Chandigarh	4,086	6	0.1
28.	D&N Haveli	222	5	2.2
29.	Daman & Diu	236	5	2.1
30.	Delhi	50,798	1,160	2.3
31.	Lakshadweep	359	163	45.4
32.	Pondicherry	1,866	63	3.4

The inadequate representation or, rather, complete absence of minorities in functional police groups leads to the total lack of understanding of their point of view and, in many cases, to a hostile reaction by the police. There have been persistent demands from various quarters to provide adequate representation to the minorities in the police, especially in the Armed police battalions, such as the PAC, BMP and SRP. In turn, intriguing arguments are put forward against any reservations for minorities in the police forces, not only by militant Hindu organisations but by senior police officers as well. A case study of the PAC in this matter will help us understand the dimensions and magnitude of this problem. The representation of the minorities especially Muslims, has never been more than three to four per cent in this force. A PAC battalion normally consists of eight companies. Each company has three platoons and each platoon has three sections. Generally the PAC is not split into less than section-strength. A section, which functionally comprises seven to nine men, operates in riots independently under the command of a head constable and, in most cases, without the close supervision of any officer. If we analyse the composition of the 72 sections available in a PAC battalion, we find that nearly 60 to 65 sections do not include a single Muslim. This results in a force reacting in what may be called a 'Hindu' way to a communal situation.

Those who oppose any deliberate recruitment of minorities in the PAC claim it is one of the finest armed police forces in the country. Before the advent of paramilitary forces such as BSF, ITBP or expansions of CRPF, it was the most sought after force. It was used from Kashmir to the North East and had set admirable examples wherever it was deployed. It is argued that such a fine force has been unnecessarily and erroneously maligned by vested interests, *i.e.*, communal Muslim leadership who attack the PAC with the sole object of demoralising the first obstacle to their sinister designs. These so-called defenders of the PAC would have us believe that it is only after the 1980 Idgah incident in Moradabad that any aberrations in the behaviour of the PAC, slightly tilted its sympathy in favour of the Hindus. This tilt itself, they say, is a reaction of the force to baseless allegations made against PAC and, they add in further justification, it was as an attempt by it to find friends among the Hindus who would defend it against its detractors.

It is true that the PAC, before its mutiny in 1973, had excelled in various law and order situations all over the country, especially in the North-East theatre where it was used extensively in counter-insurgency operations. But, it is also a fact that after 1960 there has hardly been a riot in U.P. where the role of the PAC has not been found to be partisan and specifically anti-Muslim by the press, social activists and/or human rights champions. The PAC never gained the confidence of the minorities who were the worst sufferers in communal situations. The Idgah incident in Moradabad (1980) was certainly the first major national exposure of the grave shortcomings in the structure and behaviour of the PAC. Emboldened by the absence of any punishment or structural changes, the PAC repeated its anti-Muslim performance year after year in almost each and every riot thereafter. The culmination was reached in 1987 in Meerut where many young Muslims were picked up by the PAC in Hashimpura and killed at two different places in Ghaziabad in a cold-blooded manner.

The Hashimpura episode should be an eye opener to those senior police officers who oppose the representation of the minorities in the police. The arguments against any reservation of seats for minorities, which they nonetheless continue to advance that are, such reservations will communalise the police force, the recruitment of constables on the basis of religion will lead to communal clashes in the barracks and policelines, and a time may come when these 'communally recruited' policemen may refuse to obey the commands of officers of a different religion and thereby threaten the discipline of the forces. What is ignored by these leaders of the police is the reality that the forces they are commanding have already been highly infected with the communal virus. The Hashimpura episode and recent police behaviour at the time of the demolition of Babri mosque at Ayodhya as well as during Surat and Mumbai riots are sufficient proof that all is not right in their house, that profound and dangerous problems plague their PAC and police personnel. If these leaders choose to ignore these facts, it can only mean that they do not want to put their houses in order and we are forced to conclude that they themselves are influenced by the same communalised beliefs which many other members of the majority community now hold.

We must remember the fate of an experiment in UP which failed only because of our inability to shed prejudices. During the widespread riots of 1980, the then Chief Minister of U.P., V.P. Singh, took a decision to raise certain battalions of the PAC as mixed battalions, with a fair representation of minorities known as Vishesh Seva Dal. When these battalions were raised, vested interests saw to it that the representation of Muslims remained at between three and four per cent, which was the case with other normal PAC battalions. The whole exercise proved futile and the result was hardly surprising. The men who kidnapped Muslim youths from Hashimpura in Meerut (1987) and killed them in a cold-blooded manner in Ghaziabad belonged to one of these very VSD battalions (41 BN) which were raised to protect the minorities and treat them fairly. The absence of minorities in the functional groups (one section in most of the armed police battalions and half section in a few of them) have led to similar criminal and non-professional aberrations in the behaviour of many other police organisations. Such examples are many but a few may be quoted here.

During the Bhagalpur riots (1989), Muslim riot victims numbering in three digits were handed over by the Army to a detachment of the Bihar Police led by an ASI. These riot victims were later found to have been killed by the deliberate negligence of their 'protectors'. During the Mumbai riots, wireless messages emanating from the police control room and police stations inciting and encouraging Hindu violent mobs were intercepted by a social activist Teesta Setalvad and published in many newspapers. Discriminatory behaviour of the police during searches, arrests and investigation were so glaring in the Bhiwandi Riots (1970) that the Judicial Commission was compelled to pass severe strictures.

Increase in the percentage of the minorities in various police organisations will help to improve the behaviour of the police in a communal riot, in two ways. First by recruiting more Muslims, Christians and Sikhs in the police, we will provide better opportunities to members of various religious groups to understand and appreciate each other's points of view. Policemen belonging to different religions living in one barrack, dining together in one *langar*, playing on one ground or performing the same duties together, will certainly develop a sense of comradeship or *esprit-de-corps* which will help them shed unfounded prejudices and beliefs regarding each other. Mere co-existence will help them to appreciate one another's religion better. Representation of minorities in the functional police groups (section, platoon or company) will have a dramatic impact on their reactions in a riot situation. A functional police group, having a fair sprinkling of various beliefs, can not show biases in its actions like arrests, use of force or treatment of detained persons, which we have found in the course of this study. The experiments of providing representation to the ethnic and racial minorities have been tried successfully in the U.S.A. and the U.K. The increase in the numbers of Black, Asian and Irish people has helped the average white U.S. or U.K. policeman get rid of many of his biases and improve his conduct while dealing with the minorities.

It is suggested that the representation of minorities in the police should be increased in proportion to their population. It should be a minimum of ten to twelve per cent of the police force. During this study, whenever a suggestion for reservations for minorities was put forward, it was strongly opposed by various levels of officers who were interviewed. Many reasons like reluctance on the part of the minorities, especially Muslims, to come forward to join the police, lack of education and backwardness were put forward for the existing situation. It was not within the scope of this study to analyse these reasons in detail or to prove any prejudices in the behaviour of the recruiting agencies which may be trying to ensure that minorities, though otherwise eligible, are not recruited. These require further probing and research. The present study only suggests increased representation of the minorities. This may either be done through reservations or developing some in-house methodologies to achieve this aim.

II. Training Interventions

Training is the foundation of the police profession. It is only with the help of training that a raw recruit is shaped into a professional policeman. Way back in 1859, the first training school for constables in Vellore (Madras Presidency) heralded an era of organised and systematic training for policemen in the country. Though the police was the first civil service of India which thought of institutional training, over the years it has become the most neglected area. Not only has it gradually acquired a secondary status in the scheme of things of the various police organisations, it has not kept abreast of the changing social conditions.

How much importance do we attach to training is clear from the fact that the majority of the members of the different state police organisations do not attend any training programme after passing out of their basic training courses. It is true for all the levels of recruitments, *i.e.*, constables, sub-inspectors, deputy superintendents of police. A constable who joins the force at the age of 18, does not normally attend any training course during rest of 35 to 40 years of service. This is true of IPS Officers also who provide the middle and top level leadership to the Indian police. After completing their basic training at the National Police Academy, these officers get exposed to very few training courses and there may be cases where officers have not attended any course after passing out of the National Police Academy.

Regular training interventions are necessary not only to make police officers at various levels, professionally more competent to discharge their duties and fulfil the tasks assigned to them, but also to help them shed their prejudices, biases in behaviour and unfounded beliefs regarding other religionists. The Gore Committee on police training observed with emphasis : "All the modern equipments and training available to the police can achieve nothing if their minds are not free from prejudices of caste, religion and parochialism". In fact the elementary purpose of basic training and subsequent training interventions should be to empower the minds of policemen to steer clear of these biases.

It is suggested that after every five to seven years and before every promotion, police officers of all ranks should be subjected to training courses with a view to give more emphasis on the study of human behaviour. The courses and modules should be designed in a manner which may help an average policeman to develop better understanding regarding different religions. He should also be helped through specially designed courses to understand various ethnic, regional or linguistic conflicts in an objective manner. The basic purpose of the training should be to make a trainee realize that after wearing *Khaki,* he ceases to be a Hindu or a

Muslim. His only allegiance remains to the Constitution and to various laws of the land. To attain these objectives the existing courses and training methodology will have to undergo relevant changes. It is suggested that eminent sociologists, psychologists and anthropologists should be associated with the developing and designing of such training courses. Subjects like secularism, the worst effects of fundamentalism and above all the importance of tolerance could be included in police training. Inputs like handling of a communal riot with detailed analysis of police failure in certain riot situations should be given due wightage in the courses designed for various levels. The essence and good points of all the religions may be taught as an important part of the police training. It will help the newly recruited policeman to understand different religions and shed unjust prejudices which he might have acquired. For senior level police officers, case studies of various important riots like Ahmedabad (1969), Bhiwandi (1970) and Bhagalpur (1989) or demolition of the Babri mosque (1992) where the police has been criticised by various commissions for their failings, may be taken up for detailed discussions. Experiences of foreign police organisations like those of the U.K. and the U.S.A. in dealing with ethnic and racial riots may also be of help to the senior level police officers. It will require a detailed and time-consuming exercise, as no effort has been made during this study to develop and suggest a model course design. Further research is suggested on this topic.

III. The Concept of Accountability

Theoretically much has been talked about fixing the responsibility of senior level functionaries of the police and the magistracy, but in practice we very rarely come across instances of such officers being punished or held responsible for their lapses. At the most, some junior level officers are placed under suspension after the outbreak of a communal riot. This act is again more of an eyewash than a sincere effort to identify and punish the real culprits. In most cases, we find an officer placed under suspension getting reinstated after the fury of public criticism subsides. Since suspension cannot be termed as punishment, it could be safely accepted that in most of the cases practically no punishment was awarded to any guilty official.

The recommendations of the Committee on Communal Aspects, set up by the National Integration Council and accepted by it at its session on 21st June, 1968, are very specific and clear, on fixing the accountability on senior officers responsible for maintaining communal harmony and peace. Some of the recommendations were:

(1) The District Magistrate and Superintendent of Police should be made personally responsible for prompt action to prevent or stop communal disturbances.

(2) Failure to take prompt and effective action should be considered as dereliction of duty and the officers concerned should be dealt with accordingly. Service rules should be amended if necessary.

(3) A system of suitable recognition of services rendered in preventing or dealing with communal disturbances should be introduced.

One of the reasons for guilty officials escaping punishment is the avoidably long time taken by various enquiry commissions and the reluctance on the part of the governments to accept even these belated findings. Normally an enquiry commission takes five to seven years to complete its job. At the time of appointment of a commission, Government specifies a time frame of three months to a year but we may not find a single example where a commission could complete its assigned task in the stipulated time frame.

There are many reasons for this, varying from non-cooperation from governments in providing men and material assistance to the commission, unwillingness on the part of the bureaucracy to render-co-operation to the commission, non-availability of witnesses and records, speed-breaker attitude of the lawyers, or the desire of a retired judge to continue to enjoy the perks as a member of the Commission for a longer period. Whatever may be the reasons, the delay frustrates any sincere effort to punish the guilty. It is an unfortunate fact that people have become skeptical about the appointment and findings of a commission. The declaration of the appointment of a commission is viewed more as an eyewash than as a sincere effort to identify the causes of the lapses and failures in the handling of a communal riot and to punish the erring officials.

We have found that even in those cases where punishment has been awarded it was disproportionately light when compared to the seriousness of the crime, and was mostly awarded to low level functionaries. Two instances will be sufficient to elaborate this point. We have seen earlier in this study that 116 Muslims were butchered at one place, Logain in Bhagalpur (1980). The district administration kept denying this incident for more than a month. The senior most officer punished for this lapse was an ASI. No senior officer got any punishment. Similar things happened in Meerut (1987). The ghastly incidents of Hashimpura and Maliyana were not considered serious enough to attract any punishment for senior officers.

It is suggested that the recommendations of the National Integration Council should be accepted in their true spirit. There should be some statutory provisions to make a District Magistrate or Superintendent of Police automatically responsible for any mishandling of a communal situation. To send the message clearly, it will be in the fitness of things that officers of particular levels who have been given the responsibility in a geographical jurisdiction should be placed immediately under suspension whenever a riot breaks out in their area. This level may be of officer-in-charge of a police station or a District Magistrate/Superintendents of Police. It is also suggested that the enquiries entrusted to Commissions of Enquiry, state CID or CBI should be time-bound and be completed within the stipulated time-frame. The findings and recommendations of these agencies should not be permitted to gather dust in secretariates but should be religiously acted upon.

IV. Participation of the People

The National Integration Council in its resolution dated 21st June, 1968, has made a very significant recommendation regarding the involvement of the people in the fight against communal riots. It has recommended that—"Citizens Committees may be constituted as consultative bodies at the State, District and Thana levels to promote and maintain communal harmony. Their function should include the holding of advance consultations with leaders of religious groups, to ensure peaceful celebrations of festivals. They should endeavour to promote joint participation by all communities in the festivals." This recommendation only emphasises the need to institutionalise participation of the people, in a manner which may make it compulsory on the part of the administration, to involve the people in the process of combating communal violence.

We find that there is no systematic or organised pattern of people's involvement throughout the country. It depends more or less on the whims and fancies of senior officers on the ground *i.e.*, the District Magistrate or the Superintendent of Police of a district or Commissioner of Police of a Commissionerate. If one officer believes in taking the co-operation of various segments of the society, he tries to involve them in the fight against communalism, he organises some peace committees or *mohalla* bodies and assigns them some tasks. Since these are not institutionalised, we may find these committees either becoming totally inactive or disbanded after the officer leaves the district.

The utility of such committees was best proved in an experiment undertaken at Bhiwandi. Bhiwandi is one of the most communally sensitive towns in Maharashtra which had witnessed very serious communal disturbances between 1970 and 1984. Suresh Khopare, took over the charge of Deputy Commissioner of Police, Bhiwandi on 11th of June, 1988. His unique experiment saved Bhiwandi, town from the flames of communal rioting even in the years of 1991-92 and 1993 which was the worst period after Independence with regard to the destruction of life and property in riots. During the time when Rathyatras were poisoning the atmosphere in and around Bhiwandi, he formed seventy mohalla committees which were named mohalla peace committees. Each committee comprised 25 members each from the Hindus and the Muslims. An officer of the rank of Sub-Inspector was appointed as a liaison officer for two to three committees. It was ensured that not only professionals like doctors and lawyers were made members of a committee but fair representation to the weaker sections like women, labourers or weavers was also given. The members of the committees performed wonderful jobs like fighting rumours, keeping vigil in their areas during odd hours, solving disputes like the size and routes of a religious procession or providing useful intelligence to police regarding trouble mongers in their areas. The result of this experiment were amazing. Even during the worst days of December, 1992, and January, 1993, Bhiwandi remained calm. In the meeting of the National Integration Council on 2nd of November, 1991, the Chief Minister of Maharashtra, Sudhakar Rao Naik, mentioned this experiment as an important reason behind the maintenance of peace and the absence of communal riots in Bhiwandi.

Recently, the Mumbai Police Commissioner had also started this experiment with the help of J.F. Ribeiro, an ex-Commissioner of Police, Mumbai and Ms. Sushobha Barve, an activist on this front. An interaction with the officers of Mumbai Commissionerate and officer bearers of mohalla Committees revealed that initially, the people were skeptical about this experiment but sustained efforts on the part of Satish Sahney, the Police Commissioner, Sanjay Pandey. Dy. Commissioner of Police, and non-officials like Sri Ribeiro and. Sushoba Barve, convinced them about the sincerity of Mumbai police. People have started associating themselves with these committees. Their involvement has helped Mumbai police to win to some extent the almost lost confidence of the minorities.

'Citizens for Peace' of Mumbai is another example of what could be achieved through the active involvement of the people in a communal riot situation. This group of Mumbai, rendered tremendous help to the police during the riots of December 1992, and January 1993. They not only kept on feeding the police control room regarding the happenings in their areas, but also did a commendable job in the field of rehabilitation of riot victims.

It is suggested that the recommendations of the National Integration Council should be accepted in such a way that people participation in combating a communal riot becomes institutionalised. A standard norm regarding the functions, powers and membership of peace committees should be evolved so that it may not be left to the mercy of individuals. If need be some statutory provisions should be incorporated in the State Police regulations or the Police Act.

REFERENCES

1. Source: *BPR&D*.

APPENDIX-A
Questionnaire for Riot Victims

Name:

Father's Name:

Religion:

Age:

Profession:

Education:

Tick the Correct Answer

1. How do you find police during communal riots?
   Friend ( ) Enemy ( ) Neutral ( )
2. Will you approach police for help during communal riots?
   Yes ( ) No ( ) Can't say ( )
3. Which force will you like to be deployed in your area during communal riots?
   Civil Police ( ) PAC ( ) CRPF ( ) Army ( )
4. What will you expect from Police during riots?
   (*a*) Firm and ruthless handling of rioters ( )
   (*b*) Firm and impartial dealing without any discrimination ( )
   (*c*) Soft pedalling ( )

APPENDIX-B

Questionnaire for Police Officials

Name:

Age:

Educational Qualifications:

Rank:

1. How will you define concept of Police Neutrality during a communal strife?
2. Have you ever noticed a communal bias in the behaviour of policemen during a communal riot? You may like to elaborate this point with some personal experiences.
3. Do you think that construction of Mandir/Mosque/ Gurudwara or a Church in a police lines or Police Station is correct?
4. Do you think that use of religious symbols like hanging of portraits/photographs of deities and gods in police offices or using of Shlokas of Gita on Police sign-boards as is the case with UP Police or performing Puja and breaking of coconuts during police functions, should be discouraged in day-to-day functioning of police?

APPENDIX-C

(Letter from George Couper, Secretary to the Chief Commissioner of Oudh (Avadh), to G.F. Edmonstone, Secretary to the Government of India, dated Lucknow, December 1st, 1857).[1]

With reference to the Chief Commissioner's letter to his Lordship the Governor General dated 14th September in which he stated that he had authorised the sum of Rs. 50,000 to be expended in an attempt to raise the Hindu population of Bareilly against the Mahommedan rebels, I am directed to submit the accompanying extract of a letter from Captain Gowan dated the 14th Ultimo from which his lordship in Council will perceive that the attempt was quite unsuccessful, and has been abandoned without the expenditure of any portion of the amount in question.

Copy of Captain Gowan's Letter:

I have been quite unsuccessful in my attempt to induce the Takoors round about here to collect together any number of men. I had been led to suppose that they were inclined to render effectual aid to Government, but find that the extent of aid goes not beyond professions of goodwill for the present and boasting of what they would do if they were backed by a well-appointed European force which force could do very well without them and would only be hampered by their presence. I have consequently not spent any money whatever and not drawn any cheques upon Government for any purpose.

REFERENCE

1. Source: *U.P. State Archives.*

APPENDIX-D

File # 379 Box # 84 POLICE DEPARTMENT, 1936

(*Uttar Pradesh State Archives*)

(Subject: Communal Representation—protest from Pt. Raghubar Dayal Bhatta Vaidya of Cawnpore received through C.Y. Chintamani against excess of Muslim elements in the police in Cawnpore City).

(1)

The Leader, Allahabad (letter Head)

May 27th, 1936.

My dear Maharaj Singh,

Still they come—here is one more

With kind regards, C.Y. Chintamani

The Hon. Sir Maharaj Singh, C.I.E.

Brookhill House, Naini Tal.

(2)

Dear Mr. Chintamani

Cawnpore May 18, 1936

I want to draw your attention towards the injustice to which Hindus of Cawnpore, a premier city in the provinces, are meted out owing to the strange running of the local police department. We who are under this regime and who have to suffer on account of it do not know for a while that whether this is the policy of the provincial Government or the local authorities are to be blessed for it. Anyhow, the number of Hindus in the police department here is so insignificant that it may well be said that minority community having usurped the majority has become all in all. In a word, instead of British Rule, Muslim rule is at Cawnpore in the police.

Sir, Cawnpore is a business centre and much of the Government taxes are drawn from Hindu businessmen. Apart from this if abundance in Hindu population, police department is to keep tranquillity and safeguard the interests and rights of all. But, within this very department which is acclaimed the protection of law and order much injustice is done to the Hindus. I have no grudge against my sister communities namely the Muslims, but I do feel the injustice done to the Hindus. The Hindus have no voice in this department and their proper rights are trampled down in the broad daylight. Their legal shares are snatched away from them and distributed to others before their very nose and their irony of fate is this that not a voice is heard against it, nay, even the demagogues who make empty voices at times keep quite (sic) in this respect. However, I am forwarding you a few facts in this behalf and hope you will do something to oblige. For the facts I may add that they speak of themselves and requires no testimony.

There are 8 police stations in all at Cawnpore. Out of these one is a railway police station and seven are in the different quarters in the city. The station officers of all these police stations except 3 are Muslims. For your information I am forwarding a list of all these stations with names of their officers.

Sl. No. Station (1)	Name of the Police Officer (2)	Name of the Station (3)
1.	Nawabganj	Mr. Abdul Rashid
2.	Colonelganj	Mr. Hadi Husain
3.	Kotwali	Mr. Suraj Prasad
4.	Anwarganj	Mr. Abdul Vasid
5.	Sisamau	Mr. Ali Jabbar
6.	Collectorganj	Mr. Indu Kumar
7.	Cantonment	Mr. Mukut Behari
8.	(Local) Railway	Mr. Mohammad Ilias

Now, out of 8 there are only 3 Hindu Police Station Officers and even from these three one is being transferred and the gentleman coming in his place is a Musalman. I clear it out I may say that the officer-in-charge of the police station Collectorganj Pt. Indu Kumar is being transferred and it is said that in his place, Mr. Hasan Asghari is coming. If it is true and I have no reason to disbelieve it at present, the number of Hindu Officers will remain only two.

I am also sending you a list of Hindu and Muslim Constables and the clerks, who note down the reports which are lodged, of all the eight thanas. A glimpse (sic) of it will reveal the truth.

This is the state of affairs in the City, for district a list is being forwarded for your kind perusal.

Now, in the end, I may (sic) appeal to you to take up this right cause of the Hindus. We look up to you and you are the only man who can by your efforts get the house set in order. I hope that you will leave no stone unturned in this respect and do justice with the cause which it requires.

Raghubar Dayal Bhatta Vaidya.

CITY

Kotwali	Incharge	Muslim
	2nd Officer	2 Hindu, 2 Muslims
Cantonment	Incharge	Hindu
	2nd Officer	Muslim
Colonelganj	Incharge	Muslim
	2nd Officer	1 Hindu, 1 Muslim
Sisamu	Incharge	Muslim
	2nd Officer	Hindu
Nawabganj	Incharge	Muslim
	2nd Officer	Hindu
Rlw. Station	Incharge	Muslim
	2nd Officer	Sikh

DISTRICT THANAS

Thana	*In-charge*	*2nd Officer*	*Head Constable*	*Clerk*
Kalyanpur	Hindu		Muslim	Muslim
Sheorajpore	Hindu	"	"	
Bhilhaur	Muslim	Muslim	"	"
Bithur	Hindu		"	"
Kakwan	Muslim		"	"
Sachendi	Muslim		"	"
Akbarpore	Hindu	Muslim	"	"
Mangalpore	Hindu	Muslim	"	"
Bhognipore	Muslim		"	"
Ghatampore	Muslim		"	"
Sajaiti	Muslim		"	"
Bindhnu	Hindu		"	"
Narval	Muslim	Hindu	"	"
Maharajpore	Muslim		"	"
Musanagar	Hindu		"	"

(*contd.*)

Dearapore	Hindu		"	"
Sikandera	Hindu		"	"
Rausulabad	Muslim	Hindu	"	"
Sheoli	Hindu		"	"
Gangner	Hindu		"	"

PESHKARS

Superintendent	Police Sub-Inspector	Muslim
	Head Constable	Muslim
	Clerk	Hindu
-do-No. 2	Head Constable	Muslim
	Clerk	Muslim
Deputy Superintendent	Head Constable	Muslim
	Clerk	Muslim
-do-No. 2	Head Constable	Muslim
	Clerk	Muslim
-do-(city)	Head Constable	Muslim
	Clerk	Muslim
Line Moharrir	Head Constable	Muslim
	Clerk	Muslim
District Police (civil)	Sub-Inspector 36 Hindus,	35 Muslims
	Head Constable	15 Hindus, 69 Muslims
	Naibs	15 Hindus, 56 Muslims

OUTPOSTS

Gwaltoli	2 Muslims
Permat	1 Muslim
Chunniganj	1 Muslim
Colonelganj Bazaria	1 Muslim

(*contd.*)

Baconganj	1 Muslim
Bansmandi	2 Muslims, 1 Hindu
Latouche Road	2 Muslims
Cooli Bazar	2 Muslims, 1 Hindu
Coupergunj	1 Muslim
Mac Roberiganj	1 Muslim
Juhi	3 Muslims
Nawabganj	1 Muslim
Benajhabar	1 Muslim
Cawnpore, old	1 Muslim
Celis Bazar	2 Muslims
Patkarpore	4 Muslims
Filkhana	2 Muslims, 1 Hindu
Hatea	1 Muslim
Chaubeygola	3 Muslims
Civil Lines	2 Muslims
Rail Bazar	2 Muslims
Gangaghat	1 Hindu
Faithfulganj	1 Muslim
Lal Kurti	2 Muslims
Mac Robertganj	1 Hindu

May 31, 1936

My dear Chintamani,

Thanks for your letter, dated May 27, 1936 and enclosure. I shall look into matter....

C.Y. Chintamani, M.L.C.

Editor-in-Chief , 'The Leader' Allahabad

Chief Secretary, will you please ask for a report and let me know 31-5-36.

I.G. Police will be asked for a report on the complaint enclosed.

H. Bomford 31/5

(Bomford asks R.A. Horton who is I.G.P., U.P.)

Confidential D.O. No. O-584/G-152 I.G.P., I.P. 22 July, 1936.

My Dear Bomford, CH. Bomford, Chief Secy to Govt. (U.P.)

Please refer to your D.O. Letter No. 307p. dated January 30, asking me for a report on the copy of a complaint made by Pandit Raghubar Dayal to Mr. C.Y. Chintamani.

1. I would first draw your attention to the noticeably objectionable tone of the Pandit's letter. In the first place, he states 'Instead of British rule, Muslim rule is at Cawnpore in the police' and later on, on the first page "The Hindus have no voice in this department and their proper rights are trampled down in the broad day-light, their legal shares (whatever these may be) are snatched away from them and distributed to others before their very nose and the irony of fate is this that not a voice is heard against it." *Prima facie* I think one may justifiably conclude that the gentleman who wrote this was not free from communal bias.

2. As to the facts; it is a fact that, in the 8 city police stations, 5 station officers are Muhammadans and 3 Hindus. This is as stated on paragraph 2 of the letter. It is also stated on that page that the Officer-in-Charge of Police Station Collectorganj was being transferred and a Mohammadan put in his place. The intention of this appears to be read with the rest of the letter to indicate that such transfer was being made in pursuance of the policy of "trampling down in broad daylight the proper rights of the Hindus". In actual fact, however, Pandit Indra Kumar, the statior officer in question, had been earmarked to officiate as Circle Inspector in place

of the local Circle Inspector who had been selected to officiate as Deputy Superintendent of Police. This was purely in accordance with the needs of the administration and, so far from any injustice being imposed on Pandit Indra Kumar, he was being selected as the best man to officiate, and the same remarks apply to the proposed selection of the Station Officer to officiate as Deputy Superintendent of Police was not received in time and the transfer has not taken place.

3. The position in the rural thanas is that, of the 20 Police Stations, 11 are In-charge of Hindu officers and 9 In-charge of Muslims. The balance, therefore, is in favour of the Hindus.

4. As regards under-officers, both in the city and in the rural Police Stations, it is a fact that Muhammedans largely predominate. That this is unavoidable will be obvious when it is borne in mind that of a total of 83 head constables in the Civil Police of the district, only 12 are Hindus and, out of a total of 67 Naiks, only 13 are Hindus. I may say that the reverse is the position in the Armed Police where Hindus predominate among the rank and file.

5. As Man Singh, the Deputy Inspector-General whom I asked to enquire into this matter, remarks, the Hindus are themselves responsible for their poor number in the police and he adds that he is thoroughly satisfied that the position in Cawnpore is not due to any favouritism on the part of superior officers but it is due to circumstances beyond their control. I would point out that this letter is the opinion of an officer, himself an Hindu, but one who, I know, disregards the communal bickering which certain interested persons would endeavour to accentuate in the police. I would particularly point out, with reference to the Pundit's letter, that the details which he gives can only have been supplied to him by some disgruntled Police Officer, and it is my opinion that, if anything were done to cause such officers to believe the communal agitation of this kind is likely to bear

fruit, then the greatest harm would be caused to police discipline.

6. As I have remarked in a former letter, Deputy Inspectors General make a special duty of remedying, so far as possible, communal disproportions where they exist. Man Singh has these instructions well in mind. I should also explain here that the preponderance of Muhammedans among under-officers in the Civil Police undoubtedly seems to be due to the universal use of Urdu in the Courts. In this, Muhammedans naturally have an advantage over Hindus when taking their departmental examinations for promotion (marginal note : Please see Paragraphs 522 and 523 of the Police Regulations), and the result is the more Muhammedans pass such examination than do Hindus. As such written examinations form but a small part of the promotion test in the Armed Police and the necessity for literacy is therein much less, matters are, to some extent, balanced by the preponderance in the Armed Police of Hindu Under Officers. Personally I can see no remedy for this until a common script is adopted throughout the province.

R.M. Horton

7. Police I.G.P. has given figures of Hindu and Muslim Head Constables—Naiks for the District. Are the provincial figures available—office H. Bomford 29/7.

8. Chief Secy, Separate provincial figures of Hindu and Muslim Head Constables and Naiks are not available, but the combined figures of head constables, Naiks and Constable are available. The number of Muslim Head Constables, Naiks and Constables on December 31, 1935 in the province was 908 (someone says in the margins: "908 should have been 15,058) and of Hindus 1,150 (someone corrects: 1.150 should have been 15,058). As regards other ranks the numbers were as follows :

		Muslims	*Hindus*
(1)	Gazetted Police Officers	34	48
(2)	Inspectors	65	94
(3)	Sergeants	Nil	Nil
(4)	Sub-Inspector	864	1077

9. H.M.M. (The Correct figures are 15,911 above)... It is, therefore, possible that the communal proportion might be improved by transfers from other districts. But, whether it is advisable in Cawnpore to stress communal differences is doubtful—Bomford.

10. Cawnpore, with its memories of an extremely serious communal riot not many years ago, requires careful watching on the question of communal proportions in the police. The facts given in the complaint are exaggerated. For instance, a majority of the Police Stations in rural areas are in charge of Hindu Officers; but I feel that if possible something should be done gradually to redress the disproportion in the lower ranks, and we might tell the I.G. with reference to paragraph 7 of his D.O. letter that we hope that the instructions to which he refers therein will be carried out as occasion permits. I imagine, however, that there are many districts in which Muslim constables preponderate over Hindus, one reason being not only that Muslim constables are more conversant with Urdu than, the Hindus but that the latter are as a whole less literate than the Muslims on admission to the Police.

11. I have already directed on another file that the question of Hindu Kotwal for Cawnpore should be considered when the next vacancy arises, there having been a succession of Muslim kotwal for, in my opinion, an unduly prolonged number of years. (Signature illegible) 11-8-36 Meerut.

APPENDIX-E

TRANSLATED FROM HINDI

Extract of the FIR lodged by Ajit Dutta, DIG of Police at Bhagalpur.

Police Station Kotwali Crime No. 86, dated 15-02-90, Section-143/188 IPC.

1. Complainant—Shri Ajit Dutta, Deputy Inspector General of Police, Rural Area, Bhagalpur.
2. Accused—Unkown 20-30 Rioters.
3. Section—Unlawful assembly with an intention to indulge in rioting and violation of Curfew Orders, Section 143/188 IPC.
4. Place of Occurrence—Mohalla Parvatti-3 KM South West from the Police Station.
5. Date of Occurrence—Dated 26-10-1989 Approximately at 8.30 A.M.
6. Date of Report—15-02-90, 8.30 Hrs.
7. Investigating Officer—S.I. Ishaq, PS Kotwali. Copy of First Information Report No. 365/288, Office of Deputy Inspr. General of Police, Rural, Bhagalpur.

To,

Officer In-charge, Kotwali

Subject—Regarding one round firing by me on 26-8-89 in Mohalla Parvatti.

On 26-10-89 I was going to Nathnagar with Ex-District Magistrate and at about 8.30 AM I saw 20-30 persons on the road in Mohalla Parvatti. At that time Bhagalpur was under curfew because of riots. But, these people were not ready to respect the Curfew. I stopped the vehicle and asked them as to why in spite of Curfew those persons were roaming on the road, they indicated towards Shahbhangi Mohalla which was across the railway line and told that Muslims are attacking from that side, on this I said that how can they expect to face the attack when they are only 20-30 and mostly unarmed. And it is your duty to remain inside your houses and leave your protection to the Police. Even on this those people were not willing to go back to their houses. And I warned them that they may have to face bullets if they violate curfew. Hearing this they started looking at me with great surprise. As if being Hindus, Police can not fire upon them.

Index